Blue was the Colour

A Tale of Tarnished Love

Andy Hamilton

FOOTBALL
SHORTS

**FOOTBALL
SHORTS**

Series curator Ian Ridley

First published by Pitch Publishing
and Floodlit Dreams, 2023

Floodlit Dreams

Pitch Publishing
9 Donnington Park,
85 Birdham Road,
Chichester, West Sussex,
PO20 7AJ
www.pitchpublishing.co.uk
info@pitchpublishing.co.uk

A CIP catalogue record is available for this book
from the British Library.

ISBN 978 1 80150 485 0

Typesetting and origination by Pitch Publishing
Printed and bound in the UK by TJ Books Ltd, Padstow, Cornwall

Introduction

CLEARLY THIS is going to be a story about football. It's about many other things as well, like love, memory, joy, corruption, community, mob violence, the media, class, hot dogs, socks and toilets. But all of these topics are going to be explored within the context of football. So, if you are someone who cannot stand our national obsession with kicking a ball between two sticks, then this might not be the book for you. Although it could make a nice Christmas gift for a football-loving relative or friend. Just a thought.

I decided to write this book because it felt timely. From the age of four, it was my dream to play football for Chelsea. Well, I turned 69 in May 2023, so that is probably not going to happen now. Not unless Chelsea suffer the biggest injury crisis in sporting history. But I can, at least, look back across 60-plus years and reflect on the changes I have observed in the game I love so much. As with all change, some has been good, some bad, some pointless, some annoying and some annoyingly pointless. A few of the changes, however, have been seismic and I will try my best to make sense of them. To do this, I will have to take you on what marketing types like to call a 'personal journey'. (Mind you, is it still 'personal' if I share it with lots of strangers?)

My journey is going to measure the distance between two matches at the same stadium featuring the same two teams, Chelsea and Newcastle United. The span between the two games is 62 years, but they might just as well be light years apart. The first match was played in 1960 between two teams whose players were each on a maximum wage of £20 per week (reduced to £17 in the summer). The second match took place in March 2022 between two teams of millionaires. One club – my club – was about to be confiscated from a Russian billionaire because his mate had decided to start a war. And because Boris Johnson needed to look tough on Russian oligarchs, except for the ones he partied with in Tuscany. The other club, Newcastle, had just been acquired by an oil-rich, autocratic nation-state that beheads opponents and murders journalists. The match received a lot of attention. Roman Abramovich's old toy was taking on Saudi Arabia's new one. It was not a pretty sight.

The match back in 1960 was the first game I ever saw. I was six and a half years old and I watched from the terraces in a state of all-consuming, heart-thumping, knee-jiggling, bladder-squeezing excitement and wonder.

I did not watch the second match. I only listened to the closing moments of the game on Radio 5 Live as I pottered around the kitchen trying to find some scissors.

This book is my attempt to map the distance between those two states of mind – from a world where Chelsea v Newcastle was, at that moment, the only thing that mattered *in the entire universe*, to one where it was less important than scissors.

Please don't get me wrong. I still love football. I still play, twice a week when possible, mostly in an advisory midfield role. But my attitude to the professional game has changed. Although I suspect it will be hard to tell how much it is the game that has changed and how much of it is me. If in doubt, I will probably blame society.

Finally, a trigger warning. Much of what I will say is serious, but there *will* be jokes. Because there is no story so serious that it cannot be improved by jokes.

A Disclaimer

THIS IS a memoir and memoirs are monetised memories. Memories are stories that you tell yourself and often inflict on others. Inevitably, the more you tell the stories, the more they change – either through error and omission, or because your brain instinctively tweaks them to make the past feel more entertaining. In other words, I accept *no responsibility whatsoever* for the accuracy of anything in this book.

I believe much of it to be approximately accurate-ish because my powers of recall remain reasonably efficient. I still do quite well when I shout the answers at students on *University Challenge*. But I accept that my memory is probably not as good as it used to be – though, to be honest, I can't really remember how good that was.

During the writing process, I have used what the legal profession calls 'best endeavours' to check facts wherever possible on Google and Wikipedia and such. Although I lost a lot of faith in Wikipedia a few years back, when it told the world that I had no legs. A friend of my son, Pip, had posted this entry 'for a laugh' and it stayed up there for several weeks. I had no idea that this lie was abroad until I was about to tour with a one-man show and my manager rang, perplexed at why the theatres kept asking if I would be needing a ramp.

Of course, many of the details that I needed to check could not be confirmed by search engines. For instance, no matter how often I typed in the question 'Which Chelsea match did I miss because I had German measles?' no results were found.

My most important resource, in terms of verification, was three people who, over the years, stood or sat alongside me at so many matches in sunshine, rain, drizzle, hail, sleet and snow. These are my brother, Peter, my cousin Johnny Trotter and my old friend from primary school, Andy Boyce. At least one of them witnessed most of the episodes I describe, and their memories do not always correspond with mine. As our late Queen so wisely reflected, 'Recollections may vary.' Where there are any discrepancies I will try to indicate them. But the question you must ask yourself is: 'Whose memory is likely to be the more reliable? Those three companions, or the professional writer who has spent the last 47 years making up stories for money?' One day, perhaps, all human beings will be born with inbuilt headcams so that their whole lives will be recorded with factual accuracy. But until then, we must all be our own unreliable narrators.

In closing this disclaimer, I should mention that the only contemporaneous documents available to me were my school exercise books, which include my write-ups of some of the games I attended. In fact, the illustration on the back of this book was drawn by a six-year-old me. It depicts Jimmy Greaves, in 1960, scoring past the Man City goalie, Bert Troutman (sic), which *definitely* happened. I looked it up on Wikipedia.

The Thunderbolt

ARE YOU the romantic type? Do you believe in love at first sight? A lot of people do, don't they? From time to time, you meet someone who says something like, 'The first moment I saw her I *knew* I was going to marry her,' and you try not to be disturbed by how much they sound like a stalker. It is possible, I suppose, that your future could appear before you in a split-second of revelation, but, in my experience, love is more subtle than that. I have never been struck by that thunderbolt of instant adoration. Well, apart from once.

The date was 5 November 1960. It was a Saturday. Saturday was the best day of any week because it was the holy day of football. No professional football was allowed to take place on Sundays because, according to the Bible, our supreme, eternal, all-powerful God got too tired if he worked a seven-day week. Consequently, the Church had decreed that, out of respect, the Sabbath should be a day of soul-draining boredom.

But Saturday was the day of magic.

I had been looking forward to this particular Saturday with growing enthusiasm because our house faced on to a Second World War bomb site and, in the weeks leading up to Guy Fawkes night, the locals would gradually construct an enormous bonfire amid the rubble and weeds, ready for the traditional festivities when the community would gather to celebrate the burning of Catholics. My mum and dad were not so keen on the massive bonfires because the heat could grow so intense that sometimes the glass in our front-room window would start to bend. Invariably, the blaze would become so fierce that someone would call out the fire brigade. Often it was my mum.

Exciting as the prospect of fireworks, fire engines and warping windows was, it would not have been the only reason for my nervous anticipation. After all, this was not going to be my first Guy Fawkes night, but I was also about to attend my first football match. Kick-off, three o'clock. Chelsea v Newcastle.

I cannot remember whether I wore a blue-and-white woollen bobble hat, as I did for thousands of matches afterwards. Nor can I remember whether I took the stiff, clunking, very noisy, wooden rattle that would earn me so many dirty looks in the years that followed. What I *do* know is that I was taken to the game by my big brother, Peter. He was 13 years old. I was six and a half. Imagine if that happened now, a 13-year-old taking a six-year-old to a football match. We would be taken into care immediately.

However, this is where I need to pause and interrogate my memory of that afternoon. I am certain that Pete was with me, but I find it hard to believe that our parents would have let me toddle off into a crowded stadium without an accompanying adult. Pete was a very conscientious and sensible older brother, but that does feel like an extraordinary display of trust on their part. However, Pete is adamant that it was just me and him – and possibly a few of his 13-year-old mates.

Of course, we have to bear in mind the attitudes of the time. In the early 1960s, mums and dads loved and nurtured their kids, but they also ignored them. The word 'parenting' had not yet been invented and children were allowed to roam free in herds, especially in Ealing comedies. At weekends and during the holidays, we got to 'play out' for most of the day, either in the nearby playground or in the middle of the road, which was huge fun. Admittedly, a few kids got knocked down, but they were the slow ones. That is called natural selection.

So perhaps, between the fuzzy recordings of our memories, Pete and I have recalled an accurate version. Our dad was definitely not with us that day. He was not especially interested in football. Although in later life he acquired a season ticket, principally, I think, because he wanted the company. Part of me cannot help wondering if we were possibly accompanied to that game by our Uncle John. He was a very kind, friendly Geordie and an ardent Newcastle fan. He would have been able to keep an eye on us because, back then, the crowds were not segregated into home and away fans. People were expected to get on or, at least, manage any disagreements without the intervention of someone wearing a tabard. There was, no doubt, the occasional fight, but it was unlikely to make it into the newspapers because hooliganism at football matches had not yet become a tabloid staple.

Well, who knows if we had an adult with us? Apart from Pete, obviously, because he is an older sibling and they always *know* everything. They are Google in human form.

We would have had to get to the ground reasonably early that day in order to get a good vantage point. In fact, I spent most of my youth getting to grounds early because I was a tiny child, knee-high to a hobbit. A small child on a crowded terrace stood little chance of seeing anything unless he found some high ground. Often I perched on the cold metal bar of one of the many crush barriers. I watched so many games like that, always returning home with a numbed arse. Sometimes I nagged my brother to let me sit on his shoulders. Pete's memory is that, for my first match, we stood on the raised concrete base of a floodlight pylon. That sounds right. To be honest, that whole afternoon is a bit of a blur to me.

The only part that I can picture with a startling immediacy is climbing the mountainous steps at the back of the towering West Terrace and then seeing, for the first time, the breathtaking panorama of the Stamford Bridge stadium laid out beneath me. I can hear the sound of that crowd – a buzzing hum, like a swarm of contented bees. I can remember being exhilarated by the sheer scale of it all. *That* was the moment when I fell in love. Bang went the thunderbolt.

The Prelude

IT WAS no accident that I fell in love in that way because the circumstances of my life had groomed me for that moment. To begin with, there was the little matter of geography. Our house was so close to the stadium that whenever the crowd roared, the sudden crescendo would make the ornaments on our mantlepiece tinkle. Even when the crowd was relatively calm, we could hear every collective gasp and sigh. From a very early age, I was fascinated by this mysterious, invisible beast that breathed its life into our house.

I was similarly intrigued by the hordes of men – and it was 99 per cent men – who would swarm past our window before a game. It would begin a few hours prior to kick-off, with a steady trickle of individuals who all seemed to be wearing exactly the same hat and coat. Gradually, the flow would increase and their steps would quicken. The road would become blocked with rows of double-parked cars. In the final minutes before kick-off, a wall of people would be striding at pace towards the ground. Some would even break into a run. I could feel the excitement in the air and I desperately wanted to be part of this advancing army.

Then there was the day-to-day social conditioning. Everyone in our road, naturally, supported Chelsea. Ifield Road is now a fairly chintzy, well-to-do street with terraced houses painted in ice-cream colours. But back then the houses only came in one colour – brick grey. Most of the tenants were large families of Irish heritage. My playmates had surnames like Kelleher, Murphy, Bryant, Tidey, Tracy, but all of them – *all* of them – supported Chelsea because why on earth would you not follow the team closest to home? That is the natural order of things. Or at least it should be. Now, I seem to constantly meet born-and-bred Londoners who support Liverpool or Manchester United. What is that about? How can these people sleep at night? I am not, by nature, an authoritarian, but I would make this kind of behaviour illegal. I digress.

The key factor in my conditioning was my big brother. Every small boy wants to do the things his big brother does, and Pete went to watch Chelsea. The kitchen walls were covered in his very fine drawings of Chelsea players in various athletic poses. I learned the names of every player in the team, although, to be honest, the Chelsea team at that time basically consisted of Jimmy Greaves plus ten others.

As an infant, I was a late walker but a very early talker. According to my mum, little old ladies who stopped to coo over me in my pram would often be startled to find themselves in a conversation. She may have been exaggerating but I was certainly extremely, annoyingly, talkative and I suspect that soon most of my talking was about Chelsea.

My early reading also revolved around them. I could immediately spot the word Chelsea in any page of dense newsprint. Every morning I would listen out for the rattle of our letterbox as the *Daily Express* was delivered. I was only interested in the back-page headlines to see if there was any mention of Chelsea. The front-page headline, as I recall, was invariably 'We Find Martin Bormann' – a claim that never turned out to be true. God knows how many poor South American farmers got misidentified as Nazi war criminals.

But being so young and so small meant that I had to make do with worshipping Chelsea from afar. By far the worst of it was the trauma of watching the scores come in on TV at twenty to five every Saturday on *Grandstand*'s infamous teleprinter. It seems inconceivable now, in this age of digital instantness, but the final scores were once slowly tapped out, live, on screen, by an arthritic typewriter. It was torture.

Say we were playing away to the mighty Wolves. You would watch the teleprinter creakily type out the results of teams in which you had no interest. After each flurry of results, it would pause, as if it was getting its breath back. Then, suddenly, it would clatter into life and type out the word 'Wolves'. Then another pause. Then it would type a number. If the number was high – above 2 – you were overwhelmed with foreboding. If it was lower, then you were filled with hope, which, in some ways, was worse. As you waited on tenterhooks, the teleprinter would idle for what felt like an eternity before it would set off typing the word 'Chelsea'. Then another tantric, tantalising hesitation, before it finally clattered out the all-important number that would decide your mood for the rest of that week.

I would often get in a terribly emotional state watching this drama unfold. Once, I got so worked up that I threw a glass of water over my cousin Kay. I can't remember the exact reason why I did it, but I know that I did it because it sometimes gets mentioned. Mind you, there are two sides to every story and maybe I was provoked in some way. Just saying, that's all.

Of course, I cannot remember precisely how Chelsea-obsessed I was because I was a very young child and they tend to lack objectivity about themselves. But something happened on my fifth birthday that gives a clue.

It was evening, as I recall. The doorbell rang and, weirdly, my family suggested that I should go and answer the door, which was not normally part of my duties. When I opened the door, there were two giants smiling down at me. At that stage

22

of my life, needless to say, anybody over 5ft 8in was classified as a giant.

The titans in question were two Chelsea players, Sylvan Anderton and Johnny Brooks. Johnny Brooks was quite a star, an inside-forward who had won three England caps, though he won those while playing for the dreaded Spurs. Sylvan Anderton was a 'hard-tackling wing-half' (a popular euphemism of the day). The two giants followed me up the stairs to our front room, where I expect I bombarded them with stupid questions. My mum's friend, Angela, who lived in the mansions overlooking Stamford Bridge and who knew many Chelsea players, had arranged the surprise. I was thrilled at having two living, breathing Chelsea stars in my house, even if neither of them was the one true god, Jimmy Greaves. But the fact that my parents went to the trouble of setting up this treat gives an idea of how one-tracked my little mind must have been.

In the end, my months of incessant lobbying paid off and *finally* I got to attend that first game. Up until that afternoon, my life had felt like a succession of false starts. I was what the Victorians used to call a 'sickly child'. In the womb, I had somehow managed to grow my hands in a highly original way. So I was born, effectively, with three thumbs (though only one of them had all its components and was fit for purpose). The thumbs issue meant quite a lot of hospital visits. I also arrived kitted out with a spinal curvature, various fused vertebrae and one eye that liked to wander off and do its own thing. That too meant more time in hospital, though at least I got to wear an eyepatch that made me look like a pirate.

On top of that, I was described as 'chesty'. If there was a cough going around, it had my name on it. At one stage, there was an oxygen tent. I have a dim memory of that, and a very clear memory – probably my first *real* memory – of having whooping cough and being terrified that if I did not snatch a breath in the next few seconds, then my head was definitely going to explode and I would die. If you are a parent who is hesitating about whether to let your child receive the MMR jab, please bear this description in mind.

There was another spell in hospital due to concussion, plus the bog-standard bouts of measles, mumps etc. Oh, and once I got a dart stuck in my forehead, although luckily that mishap only required an anti-tetanus jab. (How I got the dart in my head is a story too long for this book, but let's just say it was a health and safety nightmare.) My first months at primary school were disrupted by another spell in hospital to remove the pointless squishy thumb on my right hand. On the plus side, my subsequent return to the playground brought me my first taste of fame, as all the other kids gathered round me to stare at the gap where my thumb should have been.

So, all the home confinements and hospital stays had combined to give me the feeling that, thus far, my life had been on hold. I was desperate to get out there and experience the b-i-g wide world, and that afternoon, in that stadium, I got a sense of how wonderfully b-i-g and wide the world could be. And I was very lucky. The first game I saw was a cracker. Chelsea won 4-2 and, freakishly, all six goals were scored with headers. I've watched football for 64 years and have *never* seen that happen again.

Two weeks after going to my first game, I went to my second: Chelsea v Manchester City. This match was a *nine*-goal thriller. Chelsea won 6-3 and my idol, Jimmy Greaves, scored a hat-trick.

In my first two matches, I had seen two thumping Chelsea victories and 15 goals. I imagined that being a Chelsea supporter would always be this exciting and triumphant. The next season we were relegated.

At school, I wrote up lively match reports with idiosyncratic spelling, random capitals and numerals inexplicably written backwards. Reading them back, they are full of optimism. My sky was Chelsea blue. But at the end of my account of that very first game, the vague outline of a grey cloud starts to appear. Here is what I wrote, complete with erratic, infant spelling, in what was called 'My Work Book':

Holiday News. On Saturday I went to see Chelsea v Newcastle. Chelsea won 4-2. The scores for Chelsea where Tindal scored Three and Brabrook scored one. The Scores for Newcastle where both scorn by White. I had a nice time. I do hope Greaves will stay with Chelsea in sted of Going to another team.

A different kind of thunderbolt was about to strike.

A Very Special Friend

IT WAS an ordinary morning in June 1961. I was eating my breakfast, listening out for the rattle of the letterbox and the thud of the *Daily Express* hitting our doormat. The *Express* duly arrived. I can't remember the front-page headline; no doubt they had caught another Martin Bormann. I turned to the back page. The headline screamed 'Greaves Signs for Milan'. So I burst into tears.

An overreaction, I grant you, but at that moment my tiny life had been shattered into a million pieces.

Perhaps I need to provide some context here. I started watching Chelsea games in the 1960/61 season. During that season, Greaves scored 41 goals in 40 league games, including five against West Brom, four against Nottingham Forest and

Newcastle (away), plus three hat-tricks. The hat-trick I witnessed against Man City included his 100th league goal, making him the youngest player to pass the 100-goal mark, at the age of 20 years and 290 days. He was, quite simply, a phenomenon. And now he was off to some place called Italy.

To those who didn't see him play, it is very hard to convey what an extraordinary player Greaves was, but the statistics give you some idea. He remains the highest goalscorer in the history of English top-flight football with 357 goals. He is the greatest goalscorer our game has seen. But his numbers barely get a mention on TV now because of the Premier League's stranglehold over our broadcasters. Every time I hear that deathless phrase 'in Premier League history' I have to make sure no heavy objects are within chucking distance. I have to fight the impulse to scream, 'What fucking history?! We've been playing professional football since the year 1888! The Premier League started in 1992! They didn't *invent* the fucking sport! You can't treat the year 1992 as year zero and delete the past! Who's running this thing? The fucking Khmer Rouge?!'

Or words to that effect.

Incidentally, if you think that rant was a little extreme for a matter so trivial then, with the greatest respect, you are wrong. The Premier League's revisionism is hugely significant because it represents the triumph of marketing over heritage. It's indicative of how the brand has become more important than the game.

But, returning to Jimmy Greaves, it is possible that Harry Kane – who is a wonderful player – may eventually catch Greaves' record of 357 goals in the top flight. That would be a remarkable achievement. But we should not forget that Greaves set this record on pitches that were gluepots in November, ice rinks in January, and rutted, rock-hard boneshakers in April. Furthermore, Jimmy was marked by brutal defenders who could steam through the back of a striker and receive not even the wag of a finger from the ref because that kind of tackling was considered manly.

But what made Greaves special was not merely the goals that he scored, it was the way he scored them. It was the way he moved – a silky smoothness: he was extremely rapid but, at the same time, fluid and effortless. I have never seen a player so light on his feet; his feet barely kissed the grass. Above all, he had a permanent air of relaxation and calm. You never saw him hurry or take an unnecessary touch. In short, Greaves was a thoroughbred who made Alan Shearer look like a donkey. (That looks ruder on the page than I meant it to. It's a general comparison. Greaves makes most strikers look like donkeys.)

That morning in 1961, when I learned of my idol's desertion, was the climax of many weeks of frightening rumours. In fact, I had become so fearful that I had written Jimmy a letter (c/o Stamford Bridge) imploring him to see sense and stay put. But no reply came. Jimmy had made his choice. So my new favourite was Frank Blunstone.

At the time, it felt like Jimmy's failure to respond marked the end of our special relationship. But it didn't. Because some 25 years later I had cause to write to him again. I was working on a late-night sketch show on Channel 4 called *Who Dares Wins*. (A very funny show. Look it up.) Rory McGrath had created a set of spoof celebrity interviews which always began harmlessly, but would then take an unexpected, chaotic turn. For one of these sketches we needed a footballing legend to appear as themselves. Jimmy Greaves was, by now, a TV critic who had said some very positive things about our show. So I thought, what the hell? It's worth a punt. I wrote to Jimmy (c/o London Weekend Television), only this time without any random capitals. Sadly, I did not keep a copy of that invitation, but I can remember the gist.

It went something like this.

Dear Jimmy Greaves,

This is not the first letter I have written to you. When I was six years old, I wrote advising you not to go to AC Milan – a move that you have admitted in your autobiography was a 'terrible mistake'. I am writing to you now to advise you to appear in the enclosed comedy sketch for the TV show *Who Dares Wins*. Please, Jimmy, don't make the mistake of ignoring my advice again.

Yours

Andy Hamilton (Co-Producer, *Who Dares Wins*)

The letter went in the post and I did not really expect an answer. If he didn't respond, there was always Frank Blunstone.

The weeks rolled past, the tempo of production accelerated and I had almost forgotten the letter when the phone on my desk rang and our receptionist told me that a 'Mr Bleaves' was on the line. 'Bleaves?' I didn't know anyone called 'Bleaves'. Reluctantly, and probably sounding a little irritated, I told her to put him through. My pulse quickened instantly when I heard that unmistakeable voice. My exhilaration was immense. I was *actually talking, in a grown-up way, to Jimmy Greaves.*

Jimmy was politely passing on the invitation. He said he loved the sketch and was a great fan of the show, but he felt too daunted by the prospect of performing in front of a live studio audience. I tried to persuade him that he would be fine. After all, he had played, many times, in front of 100,000 fans at Wembley, not to mention 123,000 hostile Scots at Hampden Park. But he insisted that he would get too nervous. However, he promised that he would give the show a massive plug when he did his next TV review spot. We then chatted about this and that – football mostly – for about 15 minutes. Jimmy was very easy to talk to and I quickly felt like he was someone I had known all my life – which, in a sense, he was.

A few days later, I got another phone call, only this one was from my mum. For a moment, I felt a ripple of concern. Mum did not usually ring me at work and she sounded a little thrown.

'I've been watching Jimmy Greaves on the telly,' she began. 'He's just said that everyone's got to watch his old mate Andy Hamilton's show... I didn't know you knew Jimmy Greaves.'

I explained that I had not been keeping the friendship a secret from her. I'd only spoken to him on the phone, etc. Mum's was not the only call I got that morning. Friends and family kept ringing to ask how long I had been Jimmy Greaves' 'old mate'. I played it down, tried to sound casual, but inside, I was fighting the urge to turn cartwheels. (Well, perhaps not cartwheels. They have always been beyond me. The most I ever managed was a slow, risk-averse, forward roll.)

When Jimmy Greaves died in 2021 I felt inexplicably bereft. I read all the obituaries and watched all the TV tributes that charted his journey from youthful perfection, through his battles with alcohol, to his emergence as a hugely loved TV personality. I felt that someone important had disappeared from my world. Yet, objectively, that made no sense at all. I had never met him in person. The closest I had ever got to him was on a football terrace, probably a hundred yards away. But when I look back over the many, many thousands of happy experiences in my life, there are few that can compete with the moment I discovered that Jimmy Greaves had told millions of people that I was his friend.

I did not see or hear him say it, but I know that he said it. They can never take that away from me. Over the years I have *insisted* on telling this story to a great many people, whether they wanted to hear it or not. And you just got added to the list.

The Socks

THE PROBLEM with the memories from your early childhood is that you don't really remember them at all. You just think that you do. But most of the memories are like pictures behind a gauze, snatches of some half-forgotten dream. What you *remember* is the telling of that memory, or the version of it that pleases you the most, or the version that someone else had told you.

But a few childhood memories can be authenticated because someone picked up a camera and froze that moment in time. Then, many decades later, you pick up that photo and find your childhood self staring back at you, like some visiting alien.

On the front cover of this book, there is a photo of me as a very young, very small boy with a massive-looking football at my feet. I am holding a tiny, toy trophy and wearing a Chelsea kit. The shirt appears to be an accurate version of a Chelsea shirt of the day so a few outfitters were clearly starting to catch on that there might be money to be made from football kits for children. The shorts look like an ordinary pair of generic white shorts. The socks, though, are an *exact* copy of Chelsea's socks at that time. But they were not bought in a shop; my mum knitted them. In fact, I still have them in my sock drawer. She knitted them because she loved me and because they were not commercially available. At my insistence, she also sewed a number 11 onto the back of my shirt, so that I could pass myself off as Frank Blunstone.

As you can see, I look very proud of my Chelsea strip. I probably wore it to play football in the playground that was six doors up from our house. No doubt I wore it around the home. I may even have slept in it. Yet I would never have dreamed of wearing it in the crowd at Stamford Bridge. Why not? Well, because I would have been the *only* fan dressed like that. Crowds looked much more drab back then. Yes, some fans wore brightly coloured hats and/or scarves, but to actually wear the same shirt as the players would have seemed absurd. Only the footballers wore the football shirts. That was a given. Everyone knew their place.

Had I worn the shirt as leisurewear at Stamford Bridge, the word 'flash' would have been bandied around. 'Flash' meant 'showy', 'vain', 'attention-seeking' and it was not a good word. People who were deemed to be 'flash' deserved whatever they got. At that time, individualism was still viewed with some suspicion. Nowadays, individualism is celebrated and being 'flash' can get you elected. Somewhere between that deadening post-war conformism and our modern, identity-obsessed narcissism there must be a happy medium but God knows if we will ever... I'm sorry, I appear to have gone off on one.

To be honest, even now I find it hard to escape my childhood conditioning, so I still view people decked out like their heroes as slightly ridiculous. In the late 1990s, while I was queuing at the Stamford Bridge turnstiles, I got an uncontrollable fit of the giggles when I spotted four massively obese, middle-aged men wearing tent-sized Chelsea shirts with the name 'Zola' on the back. It would have been impossible to find four human beings who looked *less* like the diminutive magician Gianfranco Zola. There was something hilarious about this galumphing quartet of Anti-Zolas. It was dissonance, that's the word. (Which, incidentally, makes it OK for me to laugh at fat people.)

So why am I getting so fired up about replica kits? Well, because I think they signify something important. Of course, it is perfectly legitimate for clubs to look to profit from the allegiance of supporters. But is it necessary for them to so *ruthlessly* exploit their fans? The kits are overpriced for garments that are often manufactured at low cost in the Far East. And since when did clubs have to promote so many different away strips? Every season most of the big teams bring out new second, third or even fourth away strips, to the extent that they start to run out of colours and have to create ones not found in Nature. Every season we see more eye-burning, synthetic, day-glo yellows, greens and pinks.

Chelsea, I am ashamed to say, are particularly guilty of this. They constantly trot out in away games wearing some monstrous combination, even when they are playing a rival team with no blue in their strip whatsoever. Historically, clubs have always sought to milk their fans, but it has now been ratcheted up to an industrial scale.

The nature of modern club ownership does not help in containing this exploitation. Without wishing to sound jingoistic, it is a fact that many of our big clubs are now owned by corrupt foreign businessmen – which is a shame because it means our own home-grown English corrupt businessmen don't get the chance to break through. Where will we find the Robert Maxwells of tomorrow?

Football clubs were always controlled by greedy, dodgy millionaires. But they were *our* greedy, dodgy millionaires. They were the *local* bigwigs and top dogs. They were constrained in how much they dared to rip off supporters who were also their neighbours. The owners might have lived in mansions behind big walls, but their prestige in the community centred around their ownership of the club. If they pissed off the fans, there would be everyday consequences. Mohammed bin Salman is unlikely to wake up in Jeddah one morning and discover that a disgruntled Geordie has put a brick through his window. (I'm not advising this kind of action, by the way. He is clearly a man who bears a grudge.)

The disconnect between owners and fans manifests itself most starkly in the pricing of tickets. The attitude of the clubs seems to be increasingly extortionate. Part of me wonders if that is sustainable. More and more, I talk to friends who have given up on the big club that they always supported and are now going to watch a local, lower-tier team where the experience feels like better value for money. If the big clubs are not careful, they will end up with crowds made up of tourists, and tourists stop coming when times get tough.

The behaviour of the top clubs would be less objectionable, perhaps, if they were honest about their cynicism. But instead, they subject us all to a barrage of touchy-feely, corporate PR bullshit masquerading as inclusiveness. The match-day announcer at Stamford Bridge greets the home team onto the pitch with the declaration 'Please welcome *your* Chelsea!' Really? Give me a break.

Some years ago, I was filming a TV sketch for Sport Relief at Stamford Bridge. It was not a match day and no fans were in the stadium, so I was surprised to see the stands decked out with banners. I questioned the liaison person from the club.

'Are those banners permanent fixtures, then?' I asked.

His tone was a fraction evasive.

'Oh, yeah, sort of. They've all been made by different fan clubs from different regions.'

I scanned the banners. Some of them were huge and highly produced. They were clearly not something that an enthusiast could knock up with a sewing machine.

'Who made that one?' I asked, pointing at a gigantic draped flag that bore the image of a smiling Roman Abramovich. Beneath the benign-looking oligarch's face, in large, shouty letters, were the words 'Roman Abramovich's Blue and White Army'.

The liaison person became very uncomfortable and said, 'I think it might be the Norfolk branch… I'd have to go away and look it up.'

'Please don't pretend something so blatantly fake is authentic,' I said, but only in my head. I should have said it out loud. Mind you, I suppose the poor fella was only doing his job.

For an adult to take a child to watch a top-flight football match now is punitively expensive. At the time that photo of me in my homemade socks was taken, I was paying sixpence to watch Chelsea matches (the equivalent of 2½ new pence). My dad was on an average wage, and sixpence represented a very small percentage of his earnings. So my childhood addiction to all things Chelsea cost my parents very little. Apart from some late-night knitting marathons for my mum.

Somewhere along the line, the people who loved the sport lost control to the people who were urging them to wake up and smell the money. There was no secret meeting where representatives of FIFA, the Illuminati, the Mafia, and Rupert Murdoch gathered to draw up a master plan to steal the soul of football. It happened, like most change, through a process of drift. Gradually, the game began to bloat with cash and float away from its roots.

Now, some may feel this perspective is simplistic and coloured by nostalgia. Some may feel, as my friends often remark, that I have become a grumpy old bastard. So in the interests of balance, I will concede that over the last six decades, not *everything* connected with football has gone in a toiletwards direction. As I am about to explain.

A Positive Development

ONE OF the upsides of so much money pouring into football has been that spectators are now far less likely to die. The design and the fabric of the stadiums has improved immeasurably so that going to watch a match is no longer a physically challenging, sometimes dangerous experience. We no longer stand for the best part of two hours exposed to the elements while intermittently being squashed, squished and propelled forwards at speed by sudden crowd surges. These days if you want to go to the toilet, then you go to the toilet. It's as simple as that. Because toilets are plentiful and accessible. People no longer have to resort to peeing through the funnel of a rolled-up newspaper. As a child, I had to do this on more than one occasion. The secret was getting the right downward angle so that the person in front of you did not end up with a wet leg. It's a shame how these old skills die out, isn't it?

For many decades, supporters paid low prices and were treated like lowlife. Eventually, something had to give.

One afternoon in April 1989 I was watching *Grandstand* when they suddenly cut live to the FA Cup semi-final between Nottingham Forest and Liverpool at Hillsborough. There seemed to be crowd trouble and the commentators could not work out what was happening. Like anyone who had spent a lot of time on football terraces, I had an ominous sense of what might be happening. The clue was the sight of fans desperately trying to climb the fences. Initially, the police had interpreted this as a possible pitch invasion and were trying to turn them back, but pitchside was always where fans headed when the crush became too much. However, in response to the problem of hooliganism, Hillsborough – like many grounds – had installed high pitchside fences. So that emergency exit no longer existed.

For those who have never watched a football match from a standing position, let me explain how it used to work. Most of the time, it was absolutely fine. But the size of the crowds could vary enormously and sometimes, if it was a big match, the stadium would fill beyond its capacity. When that happened, the fans inside could experience a highly unpleasant compression, especially in the opening stages of a match.

You would find that your body was taking a pummelling and, if the squeeze was really tight, you could find it hard to breathe. You would think to yourself, *There's no way I can get through 90 minutes of this.* Instinctively, you would lift your elbows to protect your ribcage and buy yourself a few more centimetres in which to breathe. But then, after a few minutes, you would realise that the squeeze was not quite so tight now. A few minutes more and you might find you were no longer in physical contact with several strangers at once. Gradually, at last, the physical discomfort would stop. You had your own space. The crush had eased. The crowd had slowly spread itself out, evenly, almost like water, so that there were no more dangerous pressure points.

At least, that's what used to happen at Stamford Bridge, and any other ground where the terraces were vast and open. At some stadiums, though, the terraces were divided up into smaller, boxy enclosures. At your own home ground, you quickly learned the best places to stand. Away grounds, however, could be a step into the unknown.

The only time I ever felt that I might die at a football match was at White Hart Lane some time around 1968. Chelsea were playing away that day so I had decided to trek north to watch Jimmy Greaves playing for Spurs against somebody. I *think* I went on my own. I did that sometimes. I was a strange kid.

Spurs' opponents that day must have been a reasonably big team because I remember getting there very early to nab a spot with a decent view. Some of the terracing at White Hart Lane was sub-divided into semi-enclosures by waist-high whitewashed walls. I found a spot that seemed perfect. I was actually leaning on a wall, so no tall tosser was going to stand directly in front of me today. And, to my right, there was a bit more wall to shield me from any pressure coming from that side. It was a shrewd choice. I was tucked out of harm's way.

47

But as kick-off approached, slowly, the enclosure started to fill with people. It kept filling as more and more fans tried to squeeze in from the back. The crush continued to compress. Some supporters tried to shout over their shoulders to ask the fans behind them to push back. That was always a big part of the problem. The latecomers who were trying to force their way onto the terrace could never see or hear the people they were crushing down the front. That will have been the case, for certain, at Hillsborough.

Soon, I realised I had made a serious mistake. I had trapped myself between two walls and the pressure-per-square-inch was increasing inexorably. I squirmed and wriggled to try and find myself enough space to breathe, but it was hopeless. I had to try to stick it out and hope that the crush would subside once the game got going – which is what happened, thank goodness. It would have been extremely embarrassing if I had died watching Tottenham.

Looking back, I realise that that experience was not the only time I would have been in danger at a football match, but it was the only time that I *realised* I was in danger. Quite often at Chelsea, at the final whistle, much of the North Terrace crowd would start to slowly shuffle their way through the tunnel at the back of the East Stand. You had no choice but to shuffle because you were so tightly packed together. I often had my nose pressed hard against the back of someone's hairy coat. If it got bad, my brother or my cousin held my hand to ensure I didn't get swept away. I have clear memories of my feet being off the ground on more than one occasion, yet I don't remember ever feeling at risk.

Partly, that is due to my being a kid and kids think like kids. When you are a child you don't understand how quickly things can go wrong. So I never thought, *If someone trips, or if this wall collapses, then I'm in big trouble.* Also, at that age, you presume that the adults know what they are doing, especially the ones who are in charge. So that policeman on his huge horse, who was actually making the crush worse by squeezing us all to one side, was presumably doing it for a reason. My confidence stayed intact because I had not yet registered the percentage of adults who are idiots (approx. 37 per cent). Furthermore, I trusted the crowd. I loved crowds, I still do. (At big events, obviously. Not, say, in my bathroom.) The crowd seemed to possess a wisdom, a wisdom that I had sometimes witnessed in action.

On the evening of Wednesday 8 January 1964, a very excited me went to Stamford Bridge to watch Chelsea play Spurs in an FA Cup replay. It was a massive game because Spurs were *the* team at that time. Hard to believe, I know. But in football, as in the history of mankind, empires wax and wane.

Unusually, Dad took me. Perhaps there was concern about the size of the crowd. The gates were closed very early and the official attendance figure for that night was 70,123. It was almost certainly more than that. The pressure in the crowd was especially intense and, besides, the official attendance was always an underestimate because turnstile operators would let many kids sneak through without paying. I got into dozens of games like that. Also, clubs routinely lied about the size of the crowd to decrease their tax liability. At big games, when the official attendance was announced at Stamford Bridge, the number would often be met with cynical laughter from the fans. The crowd knew how big it was. The crowd knew all sorts of things, it seemed to me. It could take collective decisions.

For instance, shortly after kick-off that night, somehow, the hive-mind decided that all the small kids needed to be moved down to the safety of the greyhound track. Suddenly, I was lifted into the air and laid flat. Then I was gently passed down over the heads of the crowd, bobbing like a cork on a sea of people. Alongside me, I could see hundreds of kids being relayed in the same way. I don't think I was shouting 'Whee!' but it did feel like some extraordinary fairground ride, as I was transferred along a conveyor belt of hands, one of hundreds of children being transported on hundreds of hands belonging to hundreds of strangers. These days, I suppose, every single one of those people would need some kind of certificate. It was a remarkable exhibition of community trust and just calling it up, now, as I write, is filling me with the memory of that enchantment.

Mind you, I attended every night game in a state of enchantment. To me, they were simply magical. The whole experience. The blaze of the floodlights illuminating the vivid green of the pitch. The primary colours of the players' kits, looking bolder and brighter. Chelsea looked bluer, Spurs' white was glowing. The banked crowd seething in the semi-darkness. The glittering sparks of light, like hundreds of fireflies, as smokers lit their matches. The wafts of tobacco smoke. The smell of hotdogs and roasted chestnuts and the sting of the cold night air. The ghostly swell of tens of thousands of people singing the old Flanagan and Allen song 'Strollin''. It was an amazing sound, as if the ocean had learned to sing. (Sadly, for some reason, the Chelsea fans stopped singing 'Strollin'' in the mid-1960s. Nowadays, of course, they just stick to the modern classics like 'A-a-a-a-h, you're shit.')

Sitting on that greyhound track, aged nine, alongside all the other kids, watching that game, hearing that crowd, that was the purest form of excitement. To me, *this* was the big, wide world and I had been given a front row seat. And, for good measure, Chelsea humiliated the overmighty Spurs by two goals to nil.

When you look at footage of, say, Liverpool's Kop in the 1960s, it is hard to believe that anyone would willingly choose to be one tiny particle in that boiling mass of humanity. We have become very different people. We now have something called 'personal space' that we regard as a right. The days when we would passively accept being crammed together are over and that is no bad thing. The risk is tiny now.

All-seater stadiums have made a massive difference. It has to be acknowledged that the creation of the seat was a crucial step in the march of civilisation because it is much harder for humans to fight sitting down. Also, when everyone's seated, it is a lot easier to spot any morons. Best of all, the introduction of all-seaters meant that short people no longer had their enjoyment ruined by tall tossers, or by medium-sized tossers with unnaturally large heads, or stupid hats.

Yet with the seats has come an intangible loss of atmosphere. To try to rectify that, some clubs have been experimenting with safe standing areas. There are critics who fear that the old problems of safety and hooliganism could return but, crucially, *these* standing spectators will be arranged in tidy rows. It won't be the free-for-all of yesteryear. Perhaps it might even be vaguely affordable for people on average incomes. Or is that just me thinking like a kid again?

The English Disease

IT WAS never inevitable that money would transform top-flight British football. In fact, there was a dangerous moment in its history when the transformation could have gone in the opposite direction. Hooliganism at matches had been a growing disfigurement since the late 1960s, and by the 1980s, match attendances had dropped dramatically as fans weighed their love of football against the risk of ending up in casualty. The game's image had become ugly and toxic. The papers labelled hooliganism 'The English Disease'. It was no such thing, of course; every nation has its hooligans, though somehow Continental yobs always manage to look more stylish.

It got to the point where crowd violence became *the* dominating story about English football. And it nearly killed the game. One night in March 1985 I was sitting in front of the telly, watching live footage from Luton's ground of a full-blown, vicious, medieval-looking riot. Unfortunately, Mrs Thatcher was doing the same thing. God knows how she ended up turning on the football. As Prime Minister, she had never shown any interest in our national game. She had probably pressed the wrong button and felt puzzled that this was not the episode of *Yes, Minister* that had been advertised. Her furious reaction was to summon all the football administrators to 10 Downing Street and tell them that she would no longer tolerate the scourge of soccer hooliganism. Something had to be done. She began pressing for a ban on all away fans and identity cards for every single football supporter.

Much of her instant response to those violent scenes was fuelled by snobbery, ignorance, fear and possibly some whisky. The sight of so many young working-class men rioting would have triggered her fear of the mob. To her eyes, they would have seemed alien and animal. It was this perspective that led to her tacit acceptance of the fabricated police version of the events at Hillsborough. She was told that the football fans had behaved like scum, which would have chimed with her prejudices. It is highly doubtful whether she would ever have had a meaningful conversation with a genuine football fan. In her home, the sporting conversations would presumably have revolved around her husband's love of golf and rugger and her son's incompetent attempts at rally driving.

If Margaret Thatcher's draconian solutions had been adopted the outcome could have been terminal. Any more disincentives would have meant even more supporters deciding to stay at home. In the end, the Prime Minister did not manage to virtually criminalise football supporters, though not for the want of trying. If she'd been able to pursue her instincts, then I suspect all football fans would have ended up wearing bells around their necks.

I can't actually recall the first time I saw any crowd violence. Mind you, you usually heard it before you saw it. Suddenly there would be the rapid thumping and drumming of feet as a fight broke out and fans scattered. Necks would crane as people tried to see where the punch-up was happening, so that they could work out the best route for evasive action. The fighting – aggro, as it became known – looked very ritualistic and usually began as skirmishes between small groups of what newsreaders call 'youths'. It nearly always involved 'youths', young men and teenagers. The only exception was Millwall's hooligan element, which seemed to be composed of men, many of them dockers.

The hour leading up to kick-off was usually the time for the violence. Much of it was bravado of the kind that young males have displayed since the days when we were all treebound apes. Any naturalist would have recognised the behaviours. Arms were spread wide and chests puffed out as the rival tribe was challenged to attack. There was a great deal of noisy taunting. Then came what Sir David Attenborough calls 'a bluff charge'. One group rushed towards the other, taking care to slam on the brakes at the last possible moment. Those being charged would back off a short distance, but all the while taunting their attackers so as not to lose face. Then would come the counter-charge, and so on.

In a way, it was almost a form of pre-match entertainment, a dark alternative to military brass bands or cheerleaders. We have to be honest with ourselves. Down through the ages, human beings have got a cheap thrill out of watching other human beings beating the crap out of each other. Go to any boxing match and watch the primitive excitement in the audience. Even respectable, middle-aged mums will be on their feet screaming blue murder.

But sometimes, with no warning, the skirmishes would turn into something much more vicious. Gaps would suddenly open up where individuals had been snatched away from their tribe and were now cowering on the ground as they were kicked by many pairs of boots. Many of the kicks were to the head. You felt sickened. But you didn't go home. You stayed on to watch the game because football fans are like that. We compartmentalise. We're prepared to ignore any moral queasiness we might feel. That is how the World Cup ended up in Qatar. And why we all watched it.

As I moved through my teens, the fighting seemed to become more frequent, more intense and – most worryingly of all – more organised. The hooligans started to use artillery. Sometimes there was even an element of preparation. In 1967 my mum came with me to watch a home cup tie against Sheffield Wednesday. We stood in the Family Enclosure – an area set aside for families – and the away fans pelted us with *sharpened* coins. Apparently, we had upset them by scoring a last-minute winner. That was the only Chelsea game that I can remember Mum attending; I'm guessing the missiles probably put her off.

The really scary development was when the violence started to involve knives. The idea that anyone could get stabbed at a football match would have once seemed inconceivable. But it soon became an ugly reality. By the time Margaret Thatcher had her evening viewing ruined, knives were yet one more factor that was driving ordinary supporters away from the terraces.

So what is the root cause of hooliganism? Is it a social or biological phenomenon? Well, I don't feel qualified to theorise, but basic intelligence has to come into it somewhere, doesn't it? I have definitely seen evidence of that.

As I mentioned earlier, my dad was not really a footie person, but around Christmas, he would sometimes take me to an away game as a present. In December 1968, he took me and my friend Andy Boyce to see Chelsea play at Filbert Street, the home ground of Leicester City. We won 4-1, since you ask. Scorers Tambling, Birchenall and Osgood (2).

We boarded the train back to Euston feeling pretty happy. However, we felt less happy when our compartment filled with some notorious figures from the Shed. (Yes, the train had a compartment, just like in an Alfred Hitchcock film. That's how long ago this was.) Among our fellow passengers was Mickey Greenaway, who was known as 'Bluebottle' I *think*, because he had a snub nose like Bluebottle in *The Telegoons*, the TV version of *The Goon Show*. With him was a notorious character called 'Eccles', presumably because he hung out with Bluebottle. In addition, there were five or six others whose identities we didn't know and who, as far as we were aware, were not named after characters created by Spike Milligan.

Their behaviour was pretty yobbish and shockingly sweary. At that time, I was a boy who didn't swear. I don't know what happened to him. I remember feeling sorry for my dad because he was trapped. He could hardly admonish so many young men about their behaviour as that would have been foolhardy. So the three of us sat quietly in the corner, trying to avoid eye contact with any of them.

I was particularly apprehensive because my friend Andy Boyce is black and, at that time, racist groups like the National Front had started to cultivate football hooligans. I phoned Andy to check my memory against his. He said he could not remember being subjected to any racist abuse, but he did remember pulling his blue-and-white scarf out from under his coat to make it clear to one and all that he was a member of the right tribe.

As the train started to nose out of Leicester Station, it entered a tunnel. One of their number decided, for no discernible reason, to lower the window slightly and lob a glass bottle into the darkness. *Bang!* There was a blinding flash. There must have been some electric cable along the wall of the tunnel and the bottle had exploded on contact. When the bottle-lobber turned around, his entire face was frosted with hundreds of tiny particles of glass. They were everywhere: in his hair, his eyebrows, all over his skin. He looked as if his entire head and shoulders had been dipped in sugar. Small flecks of blood were starting to appear on his cheeks as he stared, trance-like into the middle distance. But his stupidity was not untypical. Soon we could hear the sound of more breaking glass as, up and down the train, Chelsea fans smashed up all the windows and fittings. Several times, they pulled the emergency cord for a laugh. In the end, we were all thrown off the train at Kettering.

Like I said, basic intelligence *has* to be a factor.

Mind you, one should always guard against snap judgements. When my son Robbie was six years old, I took him to see Chelsea v Liverpool. Robbie had decided he was a Liverpool fan because Liverpool had a famous goalscorer called Robbie. *He will grow out of it*, I thought. It was a brutally cold New Year's Day – the temperature was way below zero – and, in days of yore, the match might have been postponed due to a frozen pitch. But undersoil heating meant that the players could perform with their toes feeling nice and toasty while we all froze in the stands.

A few minutes after kick-off, Chelsea scored and the entire stand erupted with a deafening roar. Little Robbie, of course, had never heard this sudden, extraordinary crescendo before and the shock, combined with the biting cold, meant that he started to cry. When half-time came, our friends headed off to fetch some warm drinks. I cuddled Robbie close to me for warmth. Then I noticed someone heading in our direction. He was climbing down over the rows of empty seats with a very intense expression. He had a shaven head and the head was decorated with many startling tattoos. He was very large with huge hams for hands. The knuckles of his hands also bore tattoos. He was clearly extremely tough, because he wasn't wearing gloves. The blaze of his stare as he approached was deeply unsettling. *Oh my god*, I thought, *this bruiser looks like trouble.* Eventually he reached our seats and I braced myself for some kind of conflict situation. I made a mental note of the nearest steward.

Now this cartoon version of a thug was leaning over us ominously.

He reached into his pocket. And pulled out … a paper bag.

'Would he like a sweetie?' he asked, in a deep vibrating rumble.

Clearly he had noticed Robbie's earlier upset and had decided to try and cheer him up with some sweets. It was an act of extreme kindness and sensitivity, yet I had written him off as some kind of Neanderthal. In that moment, I felt deeply ashamed of my snobbery. It seemed I had the same mindset as Margaret Thatcher.

Incidentally, in case you are concerned on my behalf, my son *did* grow out of his devotion to Liverpool. He became an Arsenal supporter. Needless to say, he's not in the will.

Football has always had a crowd-control problem. The game's origins lie in punch-ups between rival medieval villages as they tried to propel a pig's bladder between two points. Also, football attracts big, partisan crowds and in any crowd of a certain size you will find a tiny percentage of individuals who hate their lives and want to share their fury. There will be an even tinier percentage of psychopaths who plan their acts of violence in advance. But most of those who get characterised as yobs will grow up to be ordinary, solid citizens.

For instance, at an FA Cup semi-final in 1966, a group of us found ourselves standing next to a Sheffield Wednesday fan, a know-all triumphalist Yorkshireman who made Geoffrey Boycott look like a ray of sunshine. For 90 minutes, he told us that football was a man's game and that Chelsea were losing because they were a bunch of southern softies. As the final whistle beckoned, our friend Mickey Leach wished the Yorkshireman good luck in the final, shook him warmly by the hand and then headbutted him.

Inexcusable, I know (although the man was *fantastically* annoying). Yet young Mickey grew up to be one of the loveliest men you could ever meet, someone who was adored by all who knew him. A pillar of the community. A magistrate, no less. The truth is that most young men outgrow any anti-social behaviours. Only an extremely tiny minority of sad individuals go on to become middle-aged yobs.

Unfortunately, it appears that there may currently be something of a resurgence in football hooliganism. It was sickening and saddening, for instance, to witness the trouble at the Euros

Final at Wembley in 2021. Infamously, one of the participants was filmed with a lit flare sticking out of his naked arse. As I said, intelligence *has* to be a factor.

Peak Addiction

IF YOU are a person of a certain age who attended football matches in the 1960s in and around the London area, then it is possible that you remember me. I was that little boy who *never stopped talking.* That was me. I babbled constantly for two hours or so, perched on a stool that my brother had made for me in his school woodwork lessons.

The stool proved quite hardy, though when the crowd surged forward I would often part company from it, as it barked a lot of shins on its way down the terrace. After one such surge, I remember calling out 'Has anyone seen a stool?' and a voice calling back 'Yeah, here's your fucking stool!' I have a feeling it may have been *thrown* back to us.

My babbling was down to my adrenaline, nerves and total absorption in the match. I was an obsessive, opinionated football pundit long before that profession had been invented. After one match, I walked down Ifield Road surrounded by hundreds of disappointed Chelsea fans. As we walked, I was explaining to my friends exactly where the Blues had gone wrong and which particular defender was a moron. (It was usually Joe Kirkup. For some reason, I really had it in for him.) I was so immersed in my post-match analysis that I failed to notice the crowd part in front of me, so a lamp-post smashed me in the face. The ringing in my ears was so loud that it almost drowned out the sound of my friends' laughter. Fair enough, I suppose, it must have looked like something out of a *Tom and Jerry* cartoon.

Football was everything to me then. Nothing else mattered. (Apart, possibly, from *Bilko*.) I would do anything to feed my addiction. Once, I even got my mum to lie for me. No doubt using emotional blackmail – kids are good at that – I persuaded her to write me a note explaining how I had been too poorly to attend school the previous day. In reality, I had been to Old Trafford, Manchester to see Chelsea beat Leeds in the notorious 1970 FA Cup Final replay.

Pete had driven home through the night with me crammed into the void behind the seats of his 1964 Porsche. (My sister-in-law Sylvia was in the passenger seat. She was too tall to fold herself into that space.) I got back in the early hours, tired, elated and bent double. I didn't sleep much; my brain was still fizzing with images from the game. Then I got up and went to school.

First off, I went to the school secretary's office and handed in my mum's note explaining my absence. No one questioned anything. My cunning plan had worked. Sergeant Bilko would have been proud of me. But, halfway through the morning, I was intercepted by the deputy headmaster, Mr White – 'Chalky', as he was inevitably known. Mr White was an intimidating figure with a reputation for shredding the lies of schoolboys. He was highly intelligent and ruthlessly efficient. If they had made a film about him, he would have been played by Donald Pleasence.

'Ah, Hamilton,' he said in his distinctive nasal voice.

'Yes, sir,' I replied in my distinctive nasal voice.

'So nice to see you back on your feet. What was the nature of your ailment? Was it one of those 24-hour mystery bugs that have been going around?'

There was a mischievous, dangerous twinkle in his eye. I played a straight bat.

'Yes, sir,' I said. '24-hour bug. Lots of it about.'

Through the suggestion of a very thin smile, he said, 'And did you find that the bracing Manchester air provided a suitable pick-me-up?'

Shit. He had definitely rumbled me. I had no choice but to try and bluff it out.

'I'm… I'm sorry, Mr White,' I began, trying to sound mystified. 'I… I'm afraid I… I don't know what you mean.'

Mr White fixed me with a beady eye. Then he pushed his face very close to mine and lowered his voice.

'Don't push it,' he whispered. Then he turned and walked away, probably to seek out a Chelsea-supporting truant who did *not* have a note from their mum.

My intense addiction to football peaked in those years from 1965 to 1970. The reasons were threefold.

One: Chelsea did quite well in that period. We won a couple of trophies and might have won a few more if the players could have stayed out of the pub. In April 1965 we were on the brink of a possible treble, but then the manager, Tommy Docherty, caught a lot of the team breaking his curfew and overreacted by suspending eight key players, which effectively ended our chance of winning the First Division title. To this day, it still makes me angry. Would a written reprimand not have been sufficient?

Two: George Best came along. Enough said.

Three: there were two World Cups in that period, both glorious in their own way. The 1966 World Cup was exciting at times but, for true football fans, I think it was possibly a fraction disappointing. As with all World Cups, the people who got *really* excited were the people who didn't usually watch football. So they were thrilled by the romantic victories of plucky little North Korea (how oddly that reads now) and Nobby Stiles dancing without his teeth.

But, for the football addicts, it was a disappointment that Pelé got injured, Brazil under-performed and – I know one is not supposed to say this – that England only *really* played well in the semi-final against Portugal. The final itself was great drama, but we have to be honest and say that, clearly, Geoff Hurst's shot was not over the line and the fourth goal was illegal, given that fans were running on the pitch.

The main problem for die-hard football fans, I think, was that Alf Ramsey's team did not excite the blood. He had done a great job in assembling a highly effective unit, but the football was not that great to watch. Bobby Moore was world-class, as was Bobby Charlton. During the final itself, Alan Ball was astonishing. But fans in England knew that the side was not composed of England's finest footballers. There were better centre-backs than Jack Charlton, and better number fours than Nobby Stiles. It was an achievement, yes, for them to become world champions and they showed tremendous character, but genuine football fans craved something *more*.

At the World Cup of 1970, they got it. For starters, the quality of the football was much higher. All the major nations turned up with strong, skilful sides. The England squad contained more flair players than in 1966, though Alf Ramsey seemed reluctant to pick them. The Brazil team were fantastic, easily the most exhilarating international side I've ever seen. Best of all, however, was that this World Cup was the first to be televised *in colour*. The games were exciting enough, but somehow they seemed more exciting because of the vibrant, exotic, sun-drenched Mexican colour that came flooding out into our living rooms.

The only downside of this World Cup was that it clashed with my O Levels. The O in O Levels stood for ordinary, which makes them sound unimportant, but they were seen as crucial – the first stepping stone to further education. My teachers had told me that they expected me to perform very well and get high grades in all subjects. *Cheers*, I thought.

The big problem was that, because of the time difference, some of the televised games were finishing late at night. My mum tried to persuade me that my future was more important than, say, Brazil v Uruguay, but there was only going to be one winner there. In the end, I got seven O Levels. The grades, though, were a bit underwhelming and I actually failed Latin, which came as a shock. It cut no ice when I tried to blame Pelé.

Yet, I don't regret prioritising Pelé. He remains the greatest player I have seen, and certainly the greatest *team* player. When the ball dropped to him a few yards from goal, in that match against England, what player other than Pelé would have shown the relaxation to kill the ball stone dead and then gently roll it sideways into the path of Jairzinho, to present him with an unmissable chance? All great players look like they have plenty of time but, in that moment, Pelé seemed to make time stand still.

After 1970, though still very enthusiastic, I was never quite as engrossed or obsessed with football again. The success of that 1970 World Cup proved to be a turning point. It marked the moment when football became truly global. And when the adjective 'global' becomes attached to a noun, it rarely ends well.

Close Up and Personal

ONE SUNDAY morning in the mid-1980s I fetched up at Holland Park to play in the weekly game of football that took place in the paddock behind the Commonwealth Institute. It was a sprawling, multi-national, pick-up game that often grew to over 20 players a side. On this particular morning, I was greeted with some frustrating news.

'Oh, you've just missed Pat Nevin.'

'Pat Nevin? Was he watching?' I asked.

'No. Playing,' came the answer.

I was extremely miffed to have missed the opportunity to play alongside him, to put it mildly. Watching Pat Nevin play was pretty much the only saving grace to following Chelsea in that period. He was my hero. He was living proof that very small, highly skilful players could survive in modern football. He was an original, unique. Which was why he had joined in a kickabout at a time when most top-flight footballers had stopped mixing with ordinary mortals. Nevin was like a player from a bygone age. He should have been in black and white.

There was a time, you see, when players did not live in gated luxury estates and you could easily find yourself in close proximity to your idols. Take the day I ran away from home. It must have been during the school holidays and I was, I think, about seven years old. Dad had decided to discipline me for a misdemeanour by stopping me from attending a match. I'm not sure which match. I think it might have been England v Young England – an annual fixture where England's first team played against the wannabes. To be honest, that match was always a very tame friendly, but to me, at that age, every game was *crucially important*.

Dad's punishment of me, with hindsight, was totally deserved. What I had done was thoughtless and wrong. There is no need to go into the details. Let's just say that it involved a funeral, a large plastic dice and a piano. But, in my young, romantic mind, I had been the victim of an injustice. So I decided to run away. For the day at least. But not till after I'd had breakfast.

When I left the house that morning, Mum would have expected me to come home for lunch. As a parent, I now feel ashamed of the ordeal I must have put her through. She had to endure several hours of extreme worry and distress. Also, she had to cancel her driving test. I have a clear memory of closing the front door behind me and embracing the adventure of running away into that big, wide world where I would be free from parental tyranny. The only question was where should I run away to? I didn't know any places beyond Ifield Road – or at least none that I knew how to find. In the end, I decided to run away to somewhere that I did know how to find. I strode up Ifield Road, turned right into Fulham Road and joined all the other kids who were watching the Chelsea first team train on the forecourt at Stamford Bridge.

Yes, that is correct. On many mornings, the Chelsea team trained on the uneven, sloping, *concrete* forecourt that was the main entrance to the stadium. You can see for yourself. There is plenty of footage on the internet that will confirm this.

Often there would be cars parked in the forecourt and the players would simply play around them. We, the kids, would watch, huddled together in the stadium entrance. Sometimes we would even get to kick the ball back to our heroes. Perhaps best of all, we saw *them* doing what so many of *us* spent most of our time doing: they were having a kickabout in the playground with their mates. They were young lads larking around, sharing in-jokes, teasing each other, tussling for the ball with the competitive edge of true friends. All of this would be happening just a few yards away from us.

The players usually began their match – it was about seven-a-side – in the mid-morning and finished around lunchtime. Many of them would then head off to the nearby transport cafe where they would eat their fry-ups while being watched by dozens of adoring boys, all with their noses pressed against the window.

I hung around in the now-empty forecourt for the rest of that afternoon. Obviously what mattered was that I should not back down, even though I was now hungry, tired and in need of a toilet. My plan, such as it was, meant sticking it out all day, until I could watch that 'crucial' match in the evening. I only had to hang on till they opened the turnstiles.

At around five o'clock, players started arriving in their cars. I thought I had a memory of the Chelsea captain, Terry Venables, registering that I had been there all day and asking me if my parents knew where I was. But the more I considered it, the more I began to wonder if that was a retrospectively constructed memory. Or possibly an experience that my brain had borrowed from a friend. Anyway, what I know for a fact is that, just at the moment when my bladder was about to burst, my mum turned up, breathless and looking pale. My brother had worked out where I might be found, though that hardly made him Sherlock Holmes.

In those days, not only could I encounter my heroes close-up in the Fulham Road, but I could also see and hear them falling out of the pub at closing time, because our house was diagonally opposite the Ifield Tavern – a favourite watering hole for many of the players. Pete was soon old enough to frequent the pub (though he still had to share his bedroom with a gobby younger brother). One Saturday night he came into our bedroom, possibly a little the worse for wear, and started telling me all the gossip that he had heard from players in the Ifield. He would often pass on the content of these conversations and it seemed very unfair that I was excluded from this inner circle simply because I had been born too late and was 4ft 10in tall.

'Some transfer news,' Pete said, as he took off his socks. 'George Graham's leaving.'

What? I was appalled. We were playing well at the time and Graham was a key player. *No*, I thought, *Pete's winding me up.*

'That's not true,' I said.

''S true. George Graham's going.'

'Who told you that?

'George Graham,' said Pete. 'Fallen out with the manager. He's going to Arsenal.'

Now I *knew* Pete was talking bollocks. George Graham was a Chelsea favourite; no Chelsea favourite would ever, knowingly, sign for the despised Arsenal.

A few days later he joined Arsenal.

The extreme affluence of modern players makes it very difficult for them to have any such mundane interactions with ordinary people. This is not a criticism of the players, by the way. The players are only paid the market rates. It's not their fault that the market is insane. The players in that game against Newcastle in 1960 were grossly underpaid and undervalued. But these days the supporters know they are watching millionaires, so there is more hostility, more resentment when the millionaires underperform (or are deemed to have underperformed).

For example, in the top flight, it used to be quite common to see a player who was much loved by supporters even though it was clear that he was useless. Most teams had someone like that. Someone who played with enormous heart but who made you feel nervous whenever he got the ball. The fans would joke about how bad these players were, but the jokes were full of a genuine affection. It is unrealistic to expect that sort of bond when a player – even an average player – can earn more in a week than most spectators could hope to earn in a year or even a lifetime. Fans are no longer prepared to grant that indulgence.

The money also burdens the players with some very unrealistic expectations. They have to be 'role models'. I don't remember ever viewing players as 'role models' in the behavioural sense. Yes, of course, I wanted to *play* like Greaves (then Osgood, then Charlie Cooke), but I didn't assume that they should set some moral benchmark. Some of the modern-day pearl-clutching is, frankly, laughable. The system shovels obscene amounts of money into the pockets of very young men and then expects them to behave not like young men with obscene amounts of money but like paragons of socially-aware virtue. And who is it who is the most sensitised to the players' responsibilities as role models? Predictably, it is the clubs' PR departments, who live in constant fear of damage to their brand.

Granted, to a limited extent, kids have always copied the things they have seen on *Match of the Day*. For decades now, on thousands of park pitches, kids have been diving to claim fouls. But, again, there is little point blaming professional footballers for looking to win free kicks. The answer is to change the rules so that the risks of being caught cheating outweigh any advantage that might be gained. But in the serious areas of personal conduct, I've never quite believed the 'role models' argument.

For a start, it presumes kids are amoral and stupid. Secondly, where is the evidence? I'm not aware of any spike in attacks on touchline spectators after Eric Cantona's notorious fly-kick; nor did Luis Suárez manage to start a fashion for neck-biting.

Strange as it may sound, I feel quite sorry for modern footballers. They cannot risk contact that is unmediated. Once you factor in the spit-pit that is social media, it becomes almost impossible to imagine how a modern top-flight player could do things that normal people do. It is an extreme pressure to know that your every action is likely to be recorded on someone's phone (or your own, in the case of Kurt Zouma and his flying cat). There are a few honourable exceptions – like Marcus Rashford and Jordan Henderson, who manage to start meaningful conversations about serious topics – but for most players, any engagement with fans is restricted to short, sterile tweets that someone writes for them. Somewhere along the way, a kind of intimacy was lost. It is a shame. But big money opens up big divides.

The Winds of Change

FACED WITH the chill of reality, it is very easy to snuggle down under the warm duvet of nostalgia. I really do not want this book to feel like the prose equivalent of some L.S. Lowry painting. So, for the avoidance of doubt, let me state that there was a great deal wrong with the football I watched as a child. But I did not question the status quo because I was busy being a child. Football was giving me excitement and a sense of belonging – two things that children crave. As a result, there were many questions that did not occur to me.

For instance, in the mid-1960s, I did not ask myself why the *only* black player I had seen play on the Stamford Bridge pitch was Albert Johanneson of Leeds United. Johanneson was a speedy, skilful winger, who commentators often patronised as 'the coloured lad'. But – even though I was probably writing earnest school essays in support of Martin Luther King at the time, and even though I was watching matches alongside a black friend – Johanneson's uniqueness in English football did not make me look for the injustice behind it. Not for the first, or last, time, my addiction to the game forced any other considerations from my brain.

Mind you, at least I had the excuse of being a child. Looking back, it is remarkable how little adult discussion there was on this subject. It did not get a mention on TV or on the sports pages. The elephant in the room was not being acknowledged because it was not yet deemed to be an elephant. That's how blindingly white our football was.

Interestingly, if you watch archive footage from that period, it is noticeable that there were quite a few players who were mixed race. But their struggles were not considered and, provided their skin was light enough, they were not subjected to the same levels of condescension as Albert Johanneson.

Needless to say, there were other questions I did not think to ask myself. For instance, I never bothered to query why girls were so actively discouraged from playing football, either with boys or with each other. The inequity of it never troubled me. Girls had dolls and netball; they were fine. Nor did I understand that some of the players' nicknames had a bit of an edge to them. For instance, Peter Houseman, the very skilful Chelsea left-winger, seemed to have two nicknames – both girls' names. Some called him 'Mary'; others (me included) called him 'Molly'. The term 'Mary-Ann' was one that my dad would sometimes use about someone who he regarded as effeminate and/or possibly homosexual. It was quite a common expression. 'Mary' and 'Molly', I am fairly sure, fell into a similar category. Peter Houseman acquired that nickname because – perhaps a little unfairly – the fans saw him as a player who was a lightweight tackler, someone who was reluctant to get stuck in. That was the go-to insult of the time. At the first sign of any lack of aggression, someone got called a 'fairy' or a 'poof'.

After a shaky start to his career, Peter Houseman became a very popular and appreciated player at Chelsea, though he continued to be called 'Molly'. But, in the years to follow, many players who were perceived as different in some way found themselves on the wrong end of homophobic abuse. By the turn of the century, attitudes had liberalised – or at least that is what we told ourselves.

Graeme Le Saux, the Chelsea full-back, was a player who read the *Guardian* and sometimes went to museums, ergo, in the very tiny minds of some, he *had* to be gay. That was the rumour. And in February 1999 I and many others watched in disbelief as the Liverpool striker Robbie Fowler was allowed to weaponise that rumour. As Le Saux prepared to take a free kick, Fowler bent over and theatrically waggled his backside at him, calling him a 'poof' and urging him to 'give it to me up the arse'. Le Saux complained to the referee, the ref signalled for him to get on with the game. Fowler then waggled and pointed to his buttocks even more, Le Saux remonstrated to the referee again, and this time the ref did take some action. He booked Le Saux. Presumably for time-wasting.

I watched this sequence again recently and it is very ugly. As he got no support from the officials, Le Saux took disciplinary measures into his own hands by craftily elbowing Fowler in the head.

In the following week, Le Saux wrote to Fowler apologising for the elbow. Laughably, Fowler issued a legal statement saying that his own actions had been misinterpreted. How do you misinterpret buttock-waggling? Many years later, Robbie Fowler apologised, quite graciously, on *Football Focus*, though it would have been hard for him to continue working as a pundit if he had not. I'm not doubting his sincerity; that is merely a statement of fact.

The key element in the whole sorry episode is that, at the time, Le Saux received no sympathy from the officials or the Premier League. The FA did sweet FA, apart from charging Le Saux with bringing the game into disrepute. And this was 1999 – homophobia was already considered to be deplorable but, in professional football, it was still being appeased. Since then, football has made considerable strides in areas of social injustice. The administrators like to pretend they have driven these changes, but mostly they have been in response to societal pressures and the determination of campaign groups. Much of the change, too, seems at best presentational and hollow.

For example, there was considerable sound and fury at the World Cup in Qatar, when the England captain was prevented by FIFA from wearing an armband in support of LGBT+ rights. The FA made a lot of noise, but in reality did nothing. A modern gay Premier League footballer is quite likely to find himself playing for a team that is sponsored by a nation where homosexuality is illegal and punishable with very extreme penalties. How does that square with those shiny videos that get played to fans before matches about football being a 'game for everyone'? So far, at the time of writing, not one single current Premier League player has had the confidence to come out as gay. Clearly, no one is reassured by rainbow laces.

The Man Who Changed Everything

IT IS always difficult to identify defining moments because they don't announce themselves at the time. You only see them with hindsight. My disenchantment with professional football grew as I realised it had stopped being a game and become an industry. But when *exactly* did that transformation begin? The global impact of the 1970 World Cup was certainly a trigger, but there was another, I think, in the mid-1960s. It was the triumph of youth, epitomised when the veteran 'Wizard of the Dribble', Sir Stanley Matthews, was replaced in the national psyche by the wonderkid that was George Best.

Up until the moment when Best burst onto the scene, it is hard to imagine that anyone ever went into football with the expectation of making pots of money. The local merchants who owned the clubs had to use the wealth from their other businesses to subsidise the operation. Clubs were money pits, not money pots. As for the players, yes, some got the occasional cash backhander in a brown envelope, but not enough cash to see them retire as wealthy men. In the 1950s, many of them still had other jobs. The great Tom Finney continued to work as a plumber, although my guess is that he struggled to get much plumbing done once the customer began to chat. A few players might have achieved financial security but, for the vast majority, life was as precarious as it was for the spectators who worshipped them. All that was to change, very rapidly, in the 1960s. Crucially, the maximum wage for footballers was abolished, football became showbiz and the world of Stanley Matthews began to disappear.

Matthews had been an extraordinary footballer and national icon. He was a ball-playing crowd-pleaser who, at the same time, embodied the stoic, durable qualities that were valued in post-war Britain. The man played at the highest level until his early fifties. In total, he played for Stoke for 19 years and Blackpool for 14. He played the last of his 54 games for England at the age of 42. Astonishingly, he was voted 'Footballer of the Year' aged 48.

Go and find clips of him on the internet; he is a fascinating watch. Every full-back who faces him seems to know *exactly* what he is about to do and yet they seem powerless to stop him. They know he is going to walk the ball towards them, feint to his left – just a tiny move, a micro-twitch – and then body-swerve to his right. He darts away with such acceleration over a short distance that he is virtually unstoppable. Watching the archive of him doing this, it is noticeable how often the full-back simply falls over. The movement is so sharp that it unbalances them. I suppose that is the sign of a great player in any sport; they *make* their opponents do things they don't want to do. On YouTube there is footage of him tormenting a burly full-back in an international match against the USSR at the old Wembley Stadium. He regularly leaves the poor comrade on his arse to the accompaniment of a highly unusual noise. It is the sound of 100,000 people laughing.

On 11 May 1963, I saw Matthews playing in the flesh. I was nine. He was 48, which, in the eyes of a nine-year-old is close to being dead. Sir Stanley always attracted massive crowds, so my mum insisted that I could only attend the match if I sat in the safety of the seats with her friend, Angela. My memory is that I was not all that impressed. He had the ball quite a lot and I noticed that he didn't give it away, but he never seemed to go past anyone. He was no Frank Blunstone. Disconcertingly, he had grey, thinning hair (not much of it) and pale, spindly-looking legs; to be honest, he looked like one of my uncles. The crowd, however, adored him, so his every touch was greeted with reverent applause.

During that game, Stoke's team of old men comprehensively outplayed Chelsea's youngsters, so experience beat youth on the pitch. But, before the match, I witnessed a sad defeat for experience. I was having lunch in Angela's flat, which looked directly on to the stadium. She was friends with many of the Chelsea players but I was nonetheless surprised when there was a knock at the door and in walked Chelsea's regular left-half, Frank Upton. His arrival made me feel anxious. Kick-off was approaching. What the hell was he doing here, accepting Angela's offer of a cup of tea?

'You not playing today then, Frank? Are you injured?' asked Angela.

'No,' he replied. 'I've been dropped. They've put in the young lad, Ron Harris, to mark Matthews.'

Sir Stanley was going to be man-marked by the defender who would become known, and feared, as 'Chopper'. But Frank seemed remarkably philosophical. He was about to turn 30 and it must have been a crushing blow. He would have been gearing up to face the legendary Stanley Matthews and, at the last minute, he had been replaced by a 19-year-old. Worse still, he was having to share this awful moment with some strange kid who kept staring at him from the kitchen table.

Despite his photo being used to sell tobacco and hair cream, Matthews did not see much money during his playing career. In fact, while representing England, he was once disciplined by the FA for claiming some tea and biscuits on his expenses. For George Best, however, the cost of tea and biscuits was never going to be an issue. He earned very good money from the moment he broke into the Manchester United first team at the age of 17. Like Matthews, Best seemed to embody the age – which, in the 1960s, was fast becoming the age of *youth*.

No matter who you supported, if you were young, you idolised George Best. He was brash, showy, rebellious and explosive. Older spectators, initially at least, were more wary. You would even hear that reserve in some remarks by TV commentators. During one match, Kenneth Wolstenholme was heard to say 'Here comes Best, the barbers' nightmare.' That was a recurrent theme; the older generation seemed obsessed by his hair.

The first time I saw George Best play, he looked very small, but that was because (to quote Father Ted) he was far away. I was sat right at the top of the very steep, slightly crooked North Stand that perched on four stilts. It was the autumn of 1964, and Chelsea were top of the table. But we were apprehensive about facing Man Utd because their team had two superstars, Bobby Charlton and Denis Law. Those two proved not to be the problem; the problem was the skinny, black-haired kid who tore our defence to pieces. In the years that followed, I saw Best destroy us – and other teams – on many occasions. But it was impossible not to admire the electrifying way he wrought the destruction.

In the late 1990s, I had the thrill of meeting him. I was on holiday in the Highlands with my family, but I had to fly back down to London to attend the press launch of a film I had made for Channel 4. It was a dark comedy about corruption in football called *Eleven Men Against Eleven*. (Very funny. Got several awards. Nominated for an Emmy. Just saying, that's all.) On arrival, I sought out our publicity manager, Julie Pickford, and asked who she was expecting to attend the screening.

'Journos from all the big dailies,' she said. 'Oh, and a couple of ex-players.'

'Who?' I asked.

She checked her notes. 'Erm… George Best and Rodney Marsh.'

Politely, I told Julie that she was mad. Did she seriously think those two would actually come? But come they did. George arrived with his new bride, Alex. They looked very loved-up. Julie asked George if she could fetch him a drink.

'Yes, please,' replied George. 'I'll have a white wine in a pint mug.'

Julie laughed, but then realised he was being serious.

For 90 minutes, Mr and Mrs Best sat in the front row watching my film, and George laughed loudly right to the end. Mind you, by then he had a pint of white wine inside him, so he probably would have laughed at anything.

After the screening, Rodney Marsh quickly disappeared but George Best wanted to stay and chat. A big group formed around him as we discussed the football stories of the day. Eric Cantona had just carried out his famous kung-fu kick on a Crystal Palace yob. Everyone agreed that it was disgraceful conduct by Cantona and that the fan had it coming. There were all sorts of speculations about what was going to happen to Cantona. George expressed the view that, though very gifted, Cantona was on the slow side, so he thought Eric might take his talents north of the border to see if life was easier there.

'That's what I did when I knew I'd slowed down,' said George. 'I turned out for Hibernian.'

'But isn't Scottish football full of sadistic, brutal defenders?' I asked.

'Yes,' George replied, 'but you see them coming from a long way away.'

As I chatted with George, we were interrupted by an elderly female journalist who was working for the magazine *Reveille*. She put a Dictaphone in front of my mouth and said, 'Thirty seconds please, on why you got involved with this project.'

I gave my 30 seconds' worth of answer and then she put the Dictaphone in front of George to ask him the same question. George answered that he wasn't 'involved' with it, he'd just been invited to the viewing and had really enjoyed it.

The elderly lady stopped recording and then asked, 'And you are?'

All of us listening felt affronted on George's behalf.

'My name is George Best,' said George. The old lady looked mystified. Then, to our collective horror, he spoke the words, 'I used to be a footballer.' She hesitated for a few moments.

'Didn't... didn't you used to be quite famous?' she said. 'Could I possibly interview you?' And George said yes. He sat with her for about 20 minutes, answering questions into her Dictaphone.

I was very impressed by how gracious George was with her. Many celebrities would have felt sufficiently peeved to find some excuse to get away from someone who had not known who they were. But George gave her his time.

A few hours passed and, as at most press launches, the drink kept flowing. But I needed to get home. The next morning I had to be up at stupid o'clock to catch a flight back to Inverness and rejoin my family. I was in the process of saying my goodbyes when I suddenly felt my feet leave the ground. Someone had their arms underneath my armpits and was levering me into the air before affectionately swinging me from side to side.

'An-dy!' George was bellowing. 'Come for a drink with me and Alex in The Phene Arms! Come on!!'

Apologetically, I told George that, in normal circumstances, I would love to, but I needed to get up at the crack of dawn.

'Oh, come on!' he urged.

But I stood my ground. One hour later I sat, alone, in our house in Southfields and tried to absorb the enormity of what I had done. I had just turned down a night out on the tiles, drinking in the King's Road, with *George Best*. I was in my mid-thirties at the time. My younger self would have had me taken out and shot.

Stanley Matthews was revered because he was a disciplined genius who seemed to defy Time. George, on the other hand, was the distillation of youth. He was everything that Matthews wasn't. He was good-looking, he had great hair, he wore cool clothes, he drove a sports car, he argued with referees, he slept with Miss World. He did everything that *we* wanted to do. All young men wanted to be like him. The years of post-war austerity had come to an end, and young people had money to spend now, so the businessmen took one look at George and thought *Ker-ching*.

The rise of George Best turbo-charged the commercialisation of British football. His star quality began the marketing explosion that would eventually lead to the nonsense of Brand Beckham and CR7. In the end, all of that would probably have happened anyway but, just by being George Best, George rapidly accelerated that gold rush. That is just my opinion, of course. It would have been interesting to hear George's take on what happened in that period. Maybe I could have asked him in The Phene Arms. If I had not been such a boring old twat.

The Magic of the Cup

MOST CORRUPTION is self-inflicted. Apart from a few deranged exceptions, no person ever sets out to deliberately be cynical or unethical. What happens is that, over a period of time, the chase for money causes a series of compromises that, in turn, create an environment where you lose sight of what is quintessential. Once that happens, without realising it, you are basically sailing much too fast into a field of icebergs.

(I wonder if that was any comfort to Captain Smith of the *Titanic* at the moment he realised his mistake. Did he think, *Well, I may have killed hundreds of people, but at least I've created an enduring metaphor for the dangers of reckless short-termism?*)

Over the last few decades, the FA – who cast themselves as the guardians of our game – have gone out of their way to ram many icebergs. Perhaps the most damaging collision came in 1999, when, with one decision, they managed to sink their most prized asset: the FA Cup. At the time, it probably all made perfect sense to them. England were planning to make a bid to host the World Cup. It was important, the FA felt, to stay the right side of FIFA. If the English champions didn't participate in the World Club Championship it might upset FIFA. But the tournament was being held over two weeks in January, in South America. If they took part, Manchester United would face severe fixture congestion later in the season. So it was decided to reduce the workload for the Red Devils.

There are different versions of how the decision was reached to excuse United from taking part in the FA Cup. Many associated with the club will tell you that they were pressurised into opting out of the world's most famous knockout tournament, that they had their arm twisted by those big bullies at the FA. Others will tell you that Man Utd made it pretty clear that they would only go to South America if the FA agreed to the dispensation. Whatever the truth, it was a hugely significant moment. Manchester

United became the first Cup-holders not to defend their title. Darlington were chosen as 'lucky losers' to replace them in the draw for the third round. And the FA effectively signalled to the footballing world that the FA Cup *didn't really matter*.

Of course, the FA had already started the process of devaluing their own competition. In that same season, an edict had gone out to broadcasters that the trophy should now be called 'the FA Cup sponsored by AXA'. It was embarrassing as TV presenters battled gamely to try to get through that mouthful without it sounding like soulless bullshit. The embarrassment was further compounded by the fact that nobody knew what the hell AXA was. That might have worked to AXA's advantage, had its profile been raised by people looking them up. But the truth is, nobody cared.

(In case you're interested, AXA sell insurance. And obviously one of the prime influencers in any individual's choice of insurance company is whether they've ever sponsored a sports tournament.)

It was inevitable, perhaps, that once the lucrative Premier League began in 1992, the big clubs might start to view the FA Cup as a lower priority. Consequently, in the 1990s, they started to field weakened teams full of reserves. Now, 30 years on, even the lower league sides often do that. That is the measure of how much prestige the tournament has lost. Yet there was a time when, to use an ugly phrase, it enjoyed market dominance. Every season, the biggest crowds came out for FA Cup ties. For the benefit of younger readers, I'll try to explain why.

For thousands of football fans the FA Cup represented *hope*. The vast majority of fans supported teams who they knew had no chance of winning anything. But the FA Cup was a wonderful, chaotic free-for-all that offered the prospect of glory. The competition's history was littered with rubbish teams who had somehow fluked their way along the road to Wembley, thanks to a kind draw and the occasional barnstorming performance. Any supporter of a small club knew that – on the right day, with the help of winter weather, a blind ref, and/or a horrible pitch – their minnows could take down a big fish. Fans flocked to Cup games in the hope that they might witness a giant-killing, possibly the most exciting spectacle in any sport.

For much of my life, Chelsea have been deemed to be a giant. I have experienced the humiliation of seeing us slain by Huddersfield Town, Wigan, Barnsley, Crystal Palace (when they were in the Third Division), Leyton Orient (twice), Birmingham City, Bradford City and many more that I cannot recall at this precise moment, probably because my brain is hiding the memories away to protect me from the trauma. My first experience of this phenomenon came back in 1960, when my beloved, free-scoring First Division Chelsea lost at home 2-1 to a Fourth Division team called Crewe Alexandra. *How could that possibly happen?* I asked myself. I had never heard of this place called Crewe and it sounded like they had a girl playing for them because no boys were called Alexandra. (When you are five years old, you can't quite fathom how life can unexpectedly smack you in the face with a shovel. That was a life lesson that I first learned from following a football team.)

However, there were times, during our wilderness years in the Second Division, when Chelsea were cast as the Davids upending the Goliaths. For instance, in the 1980s, when Liverpool were steamrollering every team in sight, Chelsea knocked them out of the FA Cup *twice*. The delirium of those victories was like two bursts of sunshine in a nuclear winter of gloom. In both cases, the Chelsea players who we had seen underperform so consistently raised their games to outcompete the likes of Souness and Dalglish.

In the FA Cup, you never knew if today was going to be your day. The crowds could be huge because entire towns turned out to support their teams. In the sixth round in 1965, the Shed at Chelsea turned amber and black as it filled with most of the population of Hull. When you watch Cup ties on TV now, even when there is the prospect of a romantic upset, the teams perform in front of mocking rows of empty seats. The broadcasters do their best to hype the magnitude of the match, but the gaps in the crowd contradict them.

It seems hard to believe now, but the nation used to come to a halt on FA Cup Final Day. Such was the sense of anticipation that the live TV coverage began at breakfast time. Some years the cameras even went into the players' bedrooms to interview them when they had supposedly just woken up.

Admittedly, it was bloody boring television, but it was part of the build-up.

If you were lucky enough to get a ticket for Wembley, you could watch a man in a white coat stand on top of a tower and conduct the crowd in community singing before kick-off. Traditionally, this always climaxed with 100,000 fans singing the hymn 'Abide with Me'. I was a choirboy for seven years so, in my time, I must have sung hundreds of hymns. But none of them ever carried the emotional electricity that I experienced standing among the fans at Wembley and feeling that sound break over me.

The crowd still sings 'Abide with Me' at the Cup Final, except that you won't be able to hear them. Someone like Katherine Jenkins will have been booked to belt it out on a deafening sound system. A few decades ago, some ponytail at a marketing department meeting decided that the crowd could no longer be trusted to generate the pre-match atmosphere. Instead, they opted for a barrage of banging music transmitted at volumes that are close to illegal. Now you hear no anticipatory buzz in the crowd because it is barely worth the effort of trying to talk to your neighbour, unless you have had the foresight to bring your own megaphone.

It is interesting that the marketeers' notion of how you create excitement is so close to that of a child. Excitement equals loud noise, lots of pop music, lots of promotional videos on big screens and, of course, flames. Like pretty much every sports final in the world, the FA Cup Final teams enter the arena past machines that pointlessly belch fire into the air. It is, I think, supposed to look gladiatorial. In reality, it looks tired, clichéd and inappropriate in the context of a warming planet. But I suspect this fiery trope will persist for a while, unless some child mascot has the misfortune to be incinerated.

As for that fateful decision in 1999 to excuse Man Utd, what was the depth of reasoning behind it? The FA thought it might help England stage the World Cup, but obviously the way to achieve that was to leave envelopes full of cash in people's hotel rooms.

The other question of interest is whether the situation in 1999 might have turned out differently if the club involved had not been Manchester

United. With their dominance of the early years of the Premier League, United had all the pulling power and financial clout. To many, it seemed like the footballing authorities were a little bit scared of them. If, say, John Fashanu of Wimbledon had drop-kicked an abusive fan in front of millions of TV viewers against Crystal Palace, would he have received the same suspension as Eric Cantona? My guess is that Fashanu would have been suspended for life, or possibly executed if the FA had succumbed to pressure from the *Daily Mail*. It seems nobody at the FA had the gumption to suggest that Man Utd should participate in the World Cup Championship *and* commit to taking part in the Cup.

For the record, the FA Cup in that controversial season was won by Chelsea in the last final to be played in the old Wembley Stadium. We beat Aston Villa 1-0 in a forgettable game decided by a goalkeeping error. I was there. But it did feel like the magic had gone.

Only eight years earlier, I would have said the opposite. After a 23-year absence, Chelsea were back in a Cup Final, playing Middlesbrough. After just 43 seconds, Roberto Di Matteo smashed home an epic goal and my brother Pete and I exploded to our feet, engulfed by what was one of the loudest roars I have ever heard. As we settled back into our seats, adrenaline still pumping, my brother complained of feeling unwell. He felt dizzy, disoriented. I was faced with the appalling prospect of having to leave my seat and help him seek medical care. I might even have been expected to accompany him to a hospital. How could he do this to me?

'You'll be fine,' I told him. 'Put your head between your legs or something.'

Luckily, his dizziness soon passed, but I'm not proud of the heartless way I responded. In that moment, all those many matches where he had looked after me counted for nothing. This was the FA Cup Final, for God's sake! We had just scored after 43 seconds! The magic of the Cup was casting its spell and this was destined to be our day. So I wasn't going anywhere. Weirdly, Pete says he does not have any recollection of the incident I describe. Sad when they get to that age, isn't it?

A Never-Ending Story

AT SOME point in 2022 – or it may have been 2021, the lockdowns somehow managed to fuse time – I switched on my TV to discover that England were playing Germany in something called the Nations League (not to be confused with the League of Nations, which was the international response to the horrors of the First World War). I had been watching the game for about 30 seconds or so when a quite extraordinary event occurred.

I switched it off.

Of my own free will, I, Andy Hamilton, actually switched off the football – something that had not happened since records began. As I settled down to watch several episodes of *Better Call Saul*, I tried to take in the significance of that decision. Why had I so casually broken the habit of a lifetime? It felt like something had died inside me because I did *not care* about England taking on Germany, a contest that had waymarked my life as a football fan. But deep down I knew the cause of the disillusion: the plain truth is that there is now TOO MUCH FOOTBALL!

As a young man, I would not have been able to picture my writing those words, but then I could never have imagined that the football season would so disastrously lose its shape. It used to follow a regular, pleasing pattern. All the divisions came to a head on the last Saturday in April or the first week in May. The following Saturday saw the showpiece finale of the FA Cup Final. Then, over ten days or so, there was a brief flurry of home international matches as England, Scotland, Wales and Northern Ireland took centuries' worth of hostility out on to the football pitch. After that came a mellow summer of cricket, the occasional athletics and the delightful two-week smugfest that is Wimbledon.

By the time mid-August came around, you were itching for the new football season to start. You were mentally refreshed and brimming with expectancy as you walked towards the stadium for that opening match. How many fans today could put their hand on their heart and say they still experience that? What used to be called the close season never seems to close. All through the summer months, football continues to dominate the back pages and the airwaves. The average football fan faces any new season in a state of nervous exhaustion.

It is not just the shape of the season that has disintegrated; the footballing week has also lost any sense of rhythm. The working fans used to graft through the week in the knowledge that Saturday at three o'clock would see the moment of mental release. If they were lucky, there might also be a midweek match under floodlights to illuminate the gloom. Now they can watch a match on TV virtually every night. At the weekend, they can watch a sprawling succession of Premier League matches morning, afternoon and night, with panels of pundits chattering away in the gaps.

From a business point of view, this all makes perfect sense. Investors need to wring out every drop of revenue if they are to maximise their returns. Under the old system, there were just too many days when football was not being played – or, more importantly, not being televised. Spreading out the matches was the answer, along with expanding the existing competitions and creating pointless new ones.

The aforementioned UEFA Nations League is a prime example. In theory, it was devised to replace meaningless international friendlies. But the real reason was that UEFA saw an opportunity to hoover up some additional money and, by opting for a league format, they could cram in more paydays. Most football fans don't give a toss about the competition, which is why the England games ended up being screened on Channel 4. (Sorry, Channel 4, but that is true.) To be fair, UEFA's Champions League *has* taken root in the fans' imagination, although it has long since stopped being a league of champions. In terms of trades description, the competition should really be named 'The Top Couple of Teams from Each Country Including Some Quite Average Ones League'. We now have a situation where some self-appointed 'super-clubs' are desperate to start 'The Closed Shop of Greedy Bastards Who Never Want To Have To Qualify League'.

Surely, you might ask, if there is too much football, wouldn't we see a drop-off in demand?

Well, my hunch is that that will come. But, for the time being, demand is being constantly stimulated – or, rather, over-stimulated – by a non-stop barrage of confected hype. It sticks in my craw a little to recommend the work of another comedy writer, but there is a sketch where David Mitchell perfectly skewers the cacophony of overkill that promotes the Premier League. David strides around, as a bombastic Sky TV presenter, shouting at the camera about the 'constantly happening football!' At one point he bellows, 'The giants of Charlton take on the titans of Ipswich, thus making them both seem normal-sized.' It's a lovely piece of work. (And no, David, I'm not paying you any royalties.)

What has fundamentally changed is not merely the amount of football but the amount of *talking* about football. In days gone by, yes, you would chat to your mates about a big match that might be coming up. If your team were the victims of an incompetent referee, you might well moan to your colleagues at work on a Monday. But now you can whinge all week because an entire support industry has sprung up to keep fans 'engaged' (one of my top-ten annoyingly dishonest words). The delivery vehicles are phone-ins, febrile chatrooms, showy spats between pundits, pointlessly unenlightening post-match interviews, pointlessly unenlightening pre-match press conferences, transfer deadline day hysteria, gossip websites and meaningless furores.

This incessant, incontinent babble is fuelled by various tropes. One is the 'crisis club'. In any given week, there is one club that is deemed to be that club. As I write, funnily enough, it is Chelsea. We have lost a couple of games, our latest manager is under pressure, blah-blah-blah. Last week it was Leeds, next week it will be someone else. There has to be one, in order to keep feeding fodder into the yakkity-yak machine.

VAR has proved a huge bonus to this support industry. Before VAR, if a referee made a controversial decision, among fans and pundits alike, it would prompt protracted argument. But if VAR makes a questionable decision, you can argue about the decision *and* the very existence of VAR. No one ever sang '*Why's* the wanker in the black?' (For younger readers, refs used to wear black because it made them look more dastardly.)

My problem with this 24-hour, seven-days-a-week Babel of opinion and abuse is that it seems to be making everyone permanently angry. For some supporters, their commitment is turning into a compulsive fury. Being perpetually enraged by the perceived failure of others is not healthy. If you find this is happening to you, then you need to get out of that bunker before you find yourself blaming your whole life on Harry Maguire. You are entitled to your opinions, of course you are, but do you really need to phone into a radio programme so you can shout at Robbie Savage? You're better than that.

By coincidence, I have just noticed that my Google feed is trying to enrage me by offering links to various inflammatory rumours about what is going on at Chelsea. (Yesterday, for some reason, the algorithm seemed to think that I was a Burnley supporter, presumably because I had been researching Alastair Campbell's lifelong addiction to attention-seeking.) Now, against my better judgement, I find that I have wasted the last 20 minutes watching a video interview with Chelsea's latest part-owner, Todd Boehly. Jesus, it was a hard watch. The American talks in dead-eyed business-school jargon. He repeatedly referred to Chelsea as a 'franchise' and talked of making Chelsea 'a global club on a local scale'. What the blue fuck does that mean? It's gibberish. It makes me so mad. I'm ringing Robbie Savage right now.

Frying Pan or Fire?

BEFORE ROMAN Abramovich rocked up with his magic troika full of money, Chelsea Football Club was owned by a man called Ken Bates. You may remember him. He had a snowy-white beard that made him look a bit like Father Christmas. But that was misleading. He was considerably more money-minded than Father Christmas. And more brusque.

On one occasion, my dad was in the club's ticket office trying to make a booking for a League Cup tie against some lower-division outfit. (These games were not included in the price of our season tickets.) Dad queried why such a nondescript fixture had been priced in the most expensive category. At which point, Ken Bates stormed out of a back office and told Dad that if he didn't like it he could fuck off. Dad got the firm impression that Ken Bates was not very good at customer relations – or, indeed, relations.

Bates had bought Chelsea in 1982 as a cash deal. The price was one pound sterling, though, to be fair, he was probably overcharged. The club he purchased was in dire financial trouble. He oversaw the rebuilding of the stadium and the revival of the team's fortunes. In his 21 years in charge, he hired and fired nine managers. He also tried to cage in supporters with electrified fences, but the local council refused him permission to turn on the electricity.

I'll be honest, I never liked him – and it's not just because he told my dad to fuck off. Bates had a shtick that was all too familiar. His cultivated image as a bluff, no-nonsense, straight-talker was, I felt, mostly an excuse to insult people. He came across as a bully. Also, he was something of a carpetbagger. He had been the chairman of Oldham Athletic for five years during the 1960s (during which time he broke UN sanctions to take them on tour to racist Rhodesia) and he had become the co-owner of Wigan Athletic in 1980. His business career was the kind that has finance journalists reaching for euphemisms. The word 'investigations' crops up a lot. The British government investigated Bates's attempts to buy and control land in the Virgin Islands. In 1976, he set up a bank that folded and left thousands of investors out of pocket. He has been investigated by the Financial Services Authority for alleged undisclosed shares. After he sold Chelsea to Abramovich – at a profit of £17 million – he eventually fetched up as owner of Leeds United, where he upset everyone before selling the club to a Middle East-based private equity firm in 2012.

So, all in all, I felt quite heartened when, while travelling on the Tube in 2003, I read a headline on the back page of a fellow traveller's *Evening Standard* that told me Bates had sold Chelsea. *Good riddance*, I thought. But when I actually bought my own copy of the *Standard* (no, it wasn't free then), I began to read about this little-known but obscenely wealthy Russian oligarch, Abramovich. When I got to the part that said nobody knew the *exact* source of his extreme wealth, I do remember thinking *Uh-oh*.

At the time, there was much speculation about Abramovich. One striking rumour was that he had made many of his billions by stealing a very long train carrying a cargo of diesel fuel. The train had, apparently, just disappeared deep in some forest. It gave Chelsea fans a bit of a frisson because it felt like our new owner was a Bond villain. And at least we knew that he was *genuinely* rich. So many clubs over the years have fallen prey to 'businessmen' who have bought the clubs with money they didn't have. Or with loans secured against assets they didn't own. Too many small clubs have already been destroyed by dodgy owners. Sooner or later, a big club is going to be dragged under.

Thanks to Roman Abramovich's money, I experienced the joy of watching some wonderful players in Chelsea blue. I did what most Chelsea supporters did. If you stopped to think about it, it made you feel queasy. So you didn't stop to think about it. The same mental process will be going on, right now, in the minds of Newcastle United fans, the vast majority of whom do not condone the beheading of dissidents.

To the objective eye, all this may look like gross moral abdication. But it raises an interesting point. Ask yourself, honestly, just how much corruption are you prepared to tolerate? Because in our daily lives we are prepared to accept a background hum of routine graft. We pay cash to people in the knowledge that they will not be declaring it for tax purposes. We keep our money in banks that we know have been fined for laundering the money of Mexican drug barons. You may even have had this book delivered by an online retailer that has repeatedly been accused of underpaying and mistreating its staff. To help publicise this book, I have probably put aside any qualms and been interviewed on outlets owned by Rupert Murdoch. God knows, over the last few decades, I have done that many, many times. He has made me his bitch.

Yet, for most of us, somewhere, there is a line that we would not cross. In the case of Abramovich, Chelsea fans were prepared to watch the wonders of Eden Hazard without picturing the pitch stained red with the blood of Russian peasants. But if, for the sake of argument, Abramovich had used his wealth to fix the results of matches, that would have been seen as a step too far. Football fans, like most people, are not immoral, they are just not consistently moral.

The prospect of owning a football club has always attracted charlatans, chancers, fraudsters and major criminals. The finances of top-flight football are organised in such an insane way that they provide an ideal environment for money-laundering and backhanders (or 'unsolicited gifts', to use the correct terminology). To counter the problems caused by unethical owners and directors, we do, at least, have the protection of the 'Fit and Proper Person' test, which, I understand, someone did once fail. I think it might have been Pablo Escobar, but I'd have to go and check that.

At the time of writing, the government is apparently preparing legislation to protect clubs from unscrupulous owners – legislation that I presume will come out just before the next election. But whatever the government propose will get watered down still further, I fear, once the big money starts its lobbying. If the profits to be made in football keep getting bigger, then the sport will attract shadier and shadier club owners. Given that so many shares in clubs are held by people or entities that are not publicly identified, how can we be sure that organised crime has not already secured a stake in a British club? We like to tell ourselves that this kind of tackiness only happens in other countries, don't we? Well, unless we have real transparency, how can we be so confident of that?

There is one fundamental issue that the Abramovich era threw into high relief. Throughout the Russian's tenure, I always felt extremely nervous because my club was owned, 100 per cent, by one man. One man, moreover, who was perfectly happy to fund Chelsea's enormous debts out of his own pocket. What if something happened to him? That was the constant question in my head. What if Roman had made an ill-judged joke about President Putin's prowess at judo? What if Abramovich had got hit by a bus? (The two possibilities might not have been unconnected.)

These gloomy thoughts were not dispersed when I went filming at Stamford Bridge for Sport Relief. As I was being ushered through the upper levels of the East Stand, I noticed that every locked door was being manned by a security guard with a swipe-card. I had sat in the East Stand for nearly 20 years and could not remember seeing any such measures before. So I asked the reason for so much security.

'Mr Abramovich is concerned about getting kidnapped,' I was told. That brought home to me what a mad world Abramovich lived in – and how, to a certain extent, we had had to go and live there with him. Nobody would ever have kidnapped Ken Bates because who would have bothered to pay the ransom?

In the end, as we all know, something did happen to Abramovich and, for a moment, Chelsea teetered on the brink of total collapse. When Chelsea played Saudi-owned Newcastle in that match in March 2022, it seemed to underline the dangers of giving supreme control of clubs to single individuals or entities. Once you do that, your future hangs by the most fragile of threads.

At the heart of all this chaos lies a contradiction. Premier League clubs are potential money-making machines but, at the same time, they are vital community assets. The supporters should, by right, own a significant stake but, unfortunately, moral ownership is not recognised in contract law. When chasing votes, politicians always pay lip service to giving football back to the fans but the only people who could force this change are football supporters. We would have to vote with our wallets and boycott matches. But that would mean forgoing our football. Are we up for that? Ultimately, would the club owners really care if we stayed away? They now have other options available. During the World Cup in Qatar, some people were paid to sit in the seats and provide colour and 'atmosphere' for the cameras. Plus, of course, there is always CGI. Anything can be faked nowadays.

Whose Club is it Anyway?

MY DAUGHTER Isobel is in her twenties and, when she can, she plays football twice a week. Yet she rarely watches it, nor does she follow a particular team. So she has embraced the sport, but decided to give the tribalism a miss. How weird is that? Still, at least she didn't become an Arsenal fan.

I did try to recruit her for Chelsea. On a damp February evening in 2014, I took her to see the Blues play Sparta Prague. It was the first time she had been to a stadium to watch a game live and I thought she might enjoy the spectacle. As it turned out, there was not much spectacle to enjoy. The game was awful. The only high point came at the very end, when Chelsea brought on Eden Hazard and he scored a wonderful equaliser in injury time.

It was momentarily exciting, but not enough to get Isobel hooked.

In some ways, the most telling moment occurred before the kick-off. As we settled into our seats, I noticed there was virtually no legroom because much of the available space was taken up by bulging plastic bags bearing the Chelsea logo. We were sitting among overseas visitors who had been splashing the cash in the club shop.

The row in front of us was occupied by some very animated Chinese spectators. When the two teams walked onto the pitch our view was immediately obscured by a wall of iPads held up by tourists who wanted to film the excitement of the two teams walking onto the pitch. Very politely, we asked them to lower their iPads and they very courteously apologised. So why on earth has this less than scintillating memory lodged itself in my brain?

Well, I suppose because it brought home to me how important tourism had become. If you go to any of the major grounds on any given day, you will see crocodiles of visitors being given guided tours of the stadium, inevitably culminating in the club shop. I was once filming with Frank Lampard in the players' tunnel at Chelsea, and whenever a tour was approaching, we had to conceal Frank by encircling him with all the tallest members of our crew. If we had not done that, Frank warned, then the tourists (predominantly from the Far East) would have swarmed around him for selfies, leaving us no time to film.

The problem with tourism, though, is that the more something exists for the benefit of tourists, the more artificial it becomes. I think that is why I got so irritated by that wall of iPads. In the cold light of day, however, I wondered why I had reacted like that. Why weren't the Chinese tourists entitled to go and watch a football match? What was the basis for my annoyance? Was it purely the fact that they were foreign? Was I turning into Nigel Farage? (I met him once, by the way. That man is living proof of the existence of the male menopause.)

Recently, while grazing on Google, I came across a short video featuring interviews with ardent Chelsea supporters from as far afield as India, Colombia, Arizona, Italy, South Korea and many other places. All of the fans' faces gleamed with the obsessive love of the true supporter. Nearly all of them described how Chelsea meant *everything* to them. Due to time differences, many regularly gathered to watch games on TV, live, in the middle of the night. A very high percentage had spent a lot of time and money on trips to London to see their beloved Chelsea play in the flesh. In that sense, their commitment was far greater than mine had ever been. After all, I crossed no time zones walking a few hundred yards up the Fulham Road.

In the end, I decided that the problem was me. As it so often is. But every now and then, something happens that makes my sense of unease feel justified.

In April 2021, a small clique of so-called super clubs attempted to create a permanent cartel – the Super League, as it was rather pathetically called. As it turned out, the Super League was the Stillborn League, in no small part because fans instinctively rejected the idea of a self-appointed elite deciding to do away with commercially inconvenient notions like relegation. The supporters knew that a sport where success comes with no risk of failure was not a sport at all. For me, one of the strangest sideshows in this short-lived circus was watching the Chelsea fans who would normally be characterised as yobs being hailed as heroes because they had blockaded the entrance to Stamford Bridge in protest.

The voice of the supporters won the day and, one by one, the big clubs backed away from the idea of the Super League and blamed it all on Juventus. But the danger will not have gone away; investors can smell that there is yet more money to be made from football, especially in Asia. In China, although their top league is only 20 years old, the average gate (24,000) is already the 12th-highest in the world. After some early teething problems with corruption, gambling and match-fixing, the Chinese Super League is now starting to attract top players who are only *just* over the hill.

It does not need much imagination to see what is coming down the line. Sooner or later, there is going to be a global league. The potential rewards from TV rights and other revenue streams will be so immense that yet more wealthy owners and sponsors will be attracted. Clubs will become franchises and finally be separated from their original fanbase. In 20 – or maybe 10 – years' time, tradition will be a concept that is only a marketing tool. Sky TV will be covering the latest 'clash of the titans' between the Red Bull Chelsea Wolverines and the Shanghai Nike Killer Whales.

(Incidentally, if you think I've been a bit fanciful with the animal names there, just look at what Murdoch's marketing departments did to rugby league. They created meaningless, absurd names galore. As far as I am aware, not one rhinoceros has ever been seen on the streets of Leeds, and the Manchester suburb of Leigh is not famous for its leopards.)

Again, why is all this getting to me? Change is inevitable. People adapt and accept it. Woolwich is not full of disgruntled supporters who still see Arsenal as traitorous deserters. In years to come, there will be generations of Dons fans in Milton Keynes who have no knowledge of their connection with Wimbledon's Crazy Gang of Route One testicle-grabbers. What does it matter if clubs evolve to become global? Am I a stick-in-the-mud xenophobe? Is my inner Nigel surfacing again? Next thing I know I'll be wearing a blazer.

My sense of foreboding, I suppose, is rooted in the belief that if football clubs are completely detached from their communities, then they become a manufactured product that lacks any authenticity. Now, accurately defining authenticity is a very difficult thing to do, so I am not going to try – because that is my standard approach to anything difficult – but, even though I can't define authenticity, I know it when I see it. My fear is that football at the top level will become a fake, a knock-off, an expensive imitation of the experience it once was.

Mind you, the way world events are going it is quite possible that this gloomy prognostication of mine will never come to pass. If the eastern markets collapse because of a crippling worldwide recession that impoverishes the entire planet, then all will be well. Fingers crossed, everyone.

Treasure!

FOR QUITE a few people, the first Covid lockdown was a chapter of unexpected personal discovery. Some people discovered that their gardens had these things called birds in them. Some discovered that they did not miss their work because their job was depressing and decided not to go back to it. And I discovered that I could time-travel.

I was idly hunting for things of interest on Google when I typed in the words 'Chelsea v Newcastle 1960' and found, to my amazement, that the first match I ever attended was now resurrected on the screen of the iPad. There, in glorious, fuzzy black and white, captured in two minutes 19 seconds' worth of highlights, was a factual record of that dimly-remembered childhood epiphany. Over and over again, I watched the scratchy video of those six headed goals. Three were scored by Chelsea's centre-forward Ron Tindall, who used to play cricket for Surrey in the summer. He would struggle to do that now. Or rather, he wouldn't be allowed to do that now.

It was extremely fortunate that the first game I saw had been recorded for posterity. I had somehow always presumed that televised football did not begin until 1964 with the arrival of *Match of the Day*. But as I delved through the archive, I discovered there was tons of football on TV before then, a surprising amount of it transmitted live. All sorts of games were covered live, not just Cup Finals. Online, you can find entire international matches, league clashes, even club friendlies with exotic foreign teams. Quite a lot of the live coverage begins after the match has started. In one game, Burnley v Chelsea, circa 1959, the commentator welcomes viewers with the words 'You join us here at the start of the second half. You haven't missed much.' All of this nostalgic gold dust can be visited via YouTube or Google, on a football archive site called, for some reason, 'theheavyroller'. Sadly, by writing that last sentence, I have probably just doomed several thousand marriages.

For me, much of lockdown involved my exploring this magical treasure trove. I watched hundreds of highlights and cheerfully patriotic Pathé News reports. I saw great players who I vaguely recalled watching as a boy, only now I could see them in their prime. I watched the young version of Dave Mackay dominating games for Spurs before two broken legs had slowed him down. I watched half-remembered players of enormous skill, like Peter Broadbent of Wolves and Jimmy McIlroy of Burnley. I was thrilled to hear wonderful names I'd almost forgotten, like Dick Le Flem of Nottingham Forest and Albert Cheesebrough of Leicester City. I even got to watch legendary players I had only ever heard about, like Nat Lofthouse, Duncan Edwards and Tom Finney (who looked brilliant).

Best of all, I was able to revisit some of the games I had seen as a child and compare the idealisations of my memory with the recorded reality. Most of my Chelsea idols stood up to that evaluation quite well. Bobby Tambling, Peter Osgood and Charlie Cooke still looked pretty damned good. Joe Kirkup looked far less terrible than I remembered, which made me feel rather guilty about all the abuse that I had hurled at him.

Having watched hour after hour of archive football I'm prepared to attempt various comparisons between then – or rather, all the different thens – and now. All generalisations are dangerous (including that one), so I will do my best to avoid sweeping statements but, let's be honest, I am an opinionated person so I am probably going to fail.

Let's start with the crowds. When you watch games from the 1950s and early 1960s the first thing you notice is that, because of the terracing, the crowds *look* bigger. They look like more of a swarm and there is more spillage. You see spectators sitting on the roofs of stands, on top of advertising billboards or even in trees. At some Fulham games, fans appear to be sitting on stools along the touchline, their toes just a few inches from the field of play. But nobody seems bothered by the proximity or the clear absence of any risk assessment.

The microphones that the TV crews used seem very localised. Quite often, you hear the same individual's voice poking through. They are shouting the kind of stuff that spectators have always shouted. Encouragement. Criticism. Mockery. Jokes. What you don't hear is any effing or blinding. There are some 'bloodys', the occasional 'bugger', but no f-words. Of course, this change is not specific to football. My parents would have been shocked to hear the word fuck used as freely as it is today. The word has lost its transgressive power – that's what happens with language. Now the f-word gets used for just about anything. Gordon Ramsay uses it if he is annoyed by an omelette.

At the games in the 1950s, the singing is definitely more of the singalong variety. Portsmouth fans sing their 'Play Up Pompey' chimes, Spurs fans sing 'Glory, Glory, Hallelujah', Chelsea fans sing 'Strollin'', (which I found reassuring because my cousin Johnny didn't remember this and I was beginning to wonder if I had imagined it). Before the mid-1960s, there seems to be an absence of confrontational songs about the opposition. It's not till around 1967 that you can hear the Shed serenading away fans with 'You're going home in a London ambulance'.

There are other noticeable aspects that start to disappear in the mid-1960s. For instance, before then, a good goal by the away team is often met with polite applause, similar to what you might hear when an Australian scores a boundary at Lord's. It is very rare that you hear that kind of response at football matches now. In fact, it is so rare that, if it does happen, commentators feel the need to remark upon it.

That is not to say that the games of yesteryear contain no examples of crowd disorder. A surprising number of games are interrupted by individuals venturing onto the pitch to remonstrate with the referee and/or the opposition. For some reason, it seems to happen most regularly in Merseyside derbies. (That's not stereotyping, it's just an observation.) I only saw one shockingly violent intervention by a fan, during a match between QPR and Northampton at White City. In most cases, the solo pitch invaders look less like hooligans and more like comedy drunks. Most of them get robustly escorted from the pitch by policemen, possibly before an unfortunate trip down some police station steps.

In games from the late 1950s and early 1960s, you will witness frequent mass pitch invasions, but mostly by hordes of boys. In a very entertaining game between Fulham and Manchester United, after each Fulham goal the commentator cries 'And here come the boys!' in a period voice that Harry Enfield fans would recognise. In fact, much of the commentary is pure Harry Enfield, with quite a pronounced streak of snobbery. One commentator praises the skills of a 17-year-old Jimmy Greaves, but then describes him as 'Not the deepest of thinkers.'

In my many hours of viewing, I did not see any pitch invasions like the ones of the 1980s where full-scale battles broke out. Interestingly, I did see many examples of player dissent, especially when penalties were awarded. Sometimes, the referees even got manhandled by angry defenders, so it would be wrong to say that the culture was routinely more deferential, but the dissent always seemed to die away quite quickly.

As the 1960s progressed, though, top sides like Leeds and Liverpool started to weaponise dissent, putting referees under systematic pressure. Presumably someone looked at the stats and came to the conclusion that badgering a referee increases the chances of influencing him. Personally, if I was a ref and had the likes of Billy Bremner shouting in my face for 90 minutes, then I would definitely want to give *every* decision against his team. The Leeds manager, Don Revie, habitually moaned about the bad luck his team experienced with refereeing decisions. Perhaps there was a reason for that.

But what of the football itself, how does that compare? Well, there is no doubt that today's game is faster and more technically skilful. There is no one in those fuzzy recordings who can manipulate a ball with as much exquisite variation as, say, Kevin De Bruyne. Part of the reason for that, I think, must be down to the ball. The modern ball has a synthetic, textured surface that makes it much easier to do fancy stuff compared with the dead-weight pudding that we tried to shift through the mud of school pitches. According to the internet, that ball was no heavier than the modern ball, except when it got wet. Well, all I can say is that those balls must have been soaked 100 per cent of the time because it took a lot of force to budge them.

To this day, I maintain that my short neck is down to my having to head one of those things. Often, it felt like you were playing with something that was basically an upholstered bowling ball. Without wishing to sound immodest, I would say I have reasonably good feet, but I don't remember being able to make a ball swerve, spin or bend until well into my teens – which is roughly when the leather pudding-ball began to disappear. In case you think I'm exaggerating, let me cite the great Denis Law. He said that, as a schoolboy, if you could take a corner and kick the ball as far as the penalty spot then they put you straight into the first team.

When you watch Bobby Charlton hitting rocket-shots with that ball, you have to marvel at the technique that generated all that power – though even Charlton's shots tended not to swerve; they arrowed, fast and true. But if striking the ball was more difficult, the odds against goalscoring were shortened by the size of the goalkeepers. When watching highlights from old games you find that many of the goals look oddly unimpressive. You feel the goalie ought to have been able to get to the ball because you have grown accustomed to huge goalies with massive wingspans. Placing the ball in the corner was a lot easier back then because there was more corner to aim at. In the early 1960s, before Gordon Banks became the regular choice, England picked goalkeepers like Ron Springett, Eddie Hopkinson and the great Peter Bonetti. All of them were under six feet tall. Nowadays, I doubt if any club would even consider signing them, except possibly as mascots.

The other noticeable characteristic of bygone goalies, especially those of the 1950s, is how often they were unconscious. In game after game, forwards clattered into goalkeepers at frightening velocities. In the 1957 Cup Final, Ray Wood, the Manchester United goalkeeper, had his jaw broken by a sickening high-speed collision with Peter McParland of Aston Villa. Wood played on, but as a very dizzy and confused winger. A year earlier, the Man City keeper, Bert Trautmann, continued to play on, in goal, with a *broken neck*. It is fair to say that football did not take its duty of care that seriously back then, especially as regards goalies. During that period, goalkeepers were often jokily characterised as being 'a bit mad', but, on reflection, it is quite possible that some of them were brain-damaged.

Given that I have now watched so many hundreds of hours of old-time football under the spurious pretext of doing research, I feel the urge to make these further ten observations.

1. The players look older

It's not just the baggy shorts and knobbly knees, the players of the 1950s look old before their time. Their physiques are more spindly and their faces more lined. Many of them, of course, would have served in the Second World War and all of them grew up in a time of food rationing. But as you move into the 1960s the players become noticeably better built. There are fewer small, skinny, bandy-legged inside-forwards, fewer balding full-backs. Players look sleeker, glossier; some of them even have suntans. For health statisticians, it might make for an interesting and accurate metric of the nation's health to monitor the physical appearance of footballers. Although, I suppose the modern top-flight player inhabits a different economic universe to most of the population.

2. Defenders did not muck about

They got the ball forward early. They tended not to play out from the back – mainly, I suppose, because the state of the pitches would have turned that tactic into a lottery. When every pass equalled an act of faith, then playing tippy-tappy across the back line would have been a disaster waiting to happen.

3. Defenders were less touchy-feely

If an opponent's legs were between a defender and the ball, then those limbs fell into the category of collateral damage. Referees seemed to accept this. In terms of entertainment value it meant fewer stoppages, but a lot of legs got broken. One of the many improvements of the modern game is that a ball-player lives in less fear. He will get kicked, for sure, but his assailant is much more likely to be punished. However, the modern

defender invades his opponent's privacy
a lot more readily, particularly at corners.
In short, they are grabby. Though I have
watched many hours of Tommy Smith,
Chopper Harris, etc, I can recall very few
examples of them physically holding on
to an opponent. The only footage I saw
of Norman Hunter wrestling someone
was when Francis Lee was trying
to punch him.

At my secondary school, if you used
your hands to try to hold off or restrain
an opponent, then the games master
would blow his whistle. Now every corner
resembles some kind of slapstick farce as
defenders obsessively manhandle their
opponent. In a recent Chelsea v Arsenal
match, the Blues' defender Cucurella
(whose hair would definitely have
bothered Kenneth Wolstenholme) was so
busy strong-arming Granit Xhaka that he
kept his back to play and failed to notice
the ball gently passing a few inches behind
him on its way into the Chelsea net.

It would be interesting to see the stats on how effective all the shirt-pulling and wrestling is. My guess is that it has become a norm but doesn't actually work. Eventually, perhaps, a coach will be brave enough to put this to the test.

4. **It used to be easier playing in midfield**
One of the reasons that the games from the 1950s and early 1960s seem so entertaining is that they correspond more closely to the games we played when we were kids. One team gets the ball and attacks and then the other team does the same – end-to-end, carefree abandon. Why are the games so open? Well, it is because the midfield is, by modern standards, uncongested and uncontested.

Now, I know a little about playing midfield because that is where slow players go to hide. If the one thing you are any good at is passing the ball, then midfield is the position for you to display your craft. I have played in midfield millions of times. Annoyingly, however, my enjoyment has often been spoilt by opponents repeatedly taking the ball off me while I am weighing up my options. Had I been born in the 1930s, maybe this would have proved less of an issue.

When you watch footage of Johnny Haynes, you appreciate what a fine midfielder he was. He had vision, great skill and was an exquisite passer of a ball. Like all great players, he looks like he has so much time on the ball, but that is because he *does*. There is not the same intensity so he very rarely has rival midfielders swarming over him. To Johnny Haynes, N'Golo Kanté would have looked like a visitor from another planet. In a lot of the early Man Utd games I've watched, Bobby Charlton often accelerates unchallenged through prairies of open space.

But in the mid-1960s you see a noticeable change. Fitness levels appear to rise and suddenly teams managed by the likes

of Bill Shankly, Don Revie and Tommy
Docherty boast midfielders who seem
to be everywhere at once. Suddenly, the
midfield is the fiercest area of the pitch
and if you don't move the ball quickly,
you have no chance. And you have to be
able – and prepared – to relentlessly attack
and defend. Which, of course, is the main
reason I never got to turn professional.
I was a player 20 years behind my time.
Also, training would have clashed with
choir practice.

5. Handball was not an intellectual challenge

The rule was simple. The only judgement
the referee had to make was whether he
felt the handball had been *deliberate*.
There were no nuances to be considered
about whether it was a natural position
for a hand to be on the end of an arm.
Crucially, there were no slow-motion
replays to make every action look
intentional. I once accidentally clattered
into an old lady in an airport lounge.

Slow-motion cameras would have made
me look like a psychopath.

6. **Obstruction was a thing**
   If a player tried to usher a ball out of play
   by spreading his arms wide, sticking
   out his arse and backing away from the
   ball so that an opponent could not get
   round him, then it was not called 'using
   your body' or 'making yourself big',
   it was called a free kick. Indirect. For
   obstruction. Because the game is about
   playing the ball, not showing off how big
   you are. (This is obviously the perspective
   of a small man, but I have heard taller
   commentators than me say much the
   same thing. The legendary DJ John Peel
   put this annoying phenomenon into
   his Room 101.)

7. **Awful pitches could be fun**
   Whether it was a quagmire or an ice
   rink, a terrible pitch could often create
   a tremendous match. Combing back
   through the archives, there are countless
   games where two teams ignore seemingly

impossible conditions to produce a fantastic contest. You have to wonder whether modern players would prove as determined or adaptable. That is not a criticism; they rarely get the chance to compete in imperfect circumstances. And there was a genuine skillset needed to play on, say, a rock-hard pitch that was coated in a layer of ice. It was a test of a player's courage, technique, balance and intelligence. If you want to see some examples, check out Tranmere's 2-2 draw with Chelsea in an FA Cup tie in January 1963 (the notorious big freeze) or Manchester City's demolition of Spurs on a casino of a surface in January 1968 – a game often referred to as 'The Ballet on Ice'.

8. Unfairness can be fun

Technically, modern football is superior, but it is also more predictable. It is striking, in those vintage games, how often teams come back from three goals down and how many games are high-scoring draws. The concept of a side taking a lead and then 'shutting up shop' does not seem to exist yet. Again, you don't really see teams doing that until the mid-1960s. I blame the Italians. Or, failing that, Leeds.

Behind much of the unpredictability was the number of variables, which the modern game has mostly ironed out. The pitches, as discussed, were bad enough to disadvantage the better footballing side. Not having a level playing field was a great leveller. Another potential leveller was injury. In the days before substitutes, a game could be transformed if a side was suddenly reduced to ten men. It was very unfair, of course it was, but it often created drama. Teams could produce battling displays despite being short-staffed. Sometimes the crippled player got parked up front, where he could limp around and, if luck was with him, get to be a hero. In 1963 I saw Ian Watson – an occasional full-back for Chelsea – hobble around on one leg against Arsenal and then head the decisive goal. (It was the only goal he ever scored for us. Being kept on the pitch cannot have been that good for him, but he must have been OK because he went on to play over 200 games for QPR, which, I presume, requires the use of both legs.)

Another variable that has largely disappeared is fatigue. On those sapping pitches, the last 20 minutes of a game could become a battle of wills between two sets of tired legs and brains. If one team started to wilt, you could see an exciting swing of momentum. In a world with five substitutes, however, you are far less likely to see a team start to buckle.

Happily, a few variables persist. Human nature means that there is always the potential for a player to swing a game by doing something stupid and getting himself sent off. (Step up, David Speedie.) And notwithstanding the technologies, it is still possible for a ref to lose you a match by missing the blindingly obvious. (Yes,

David W. Smith of Stonehouse – 59 years
may have passed, but I haven't forgotten.)

9. Managers used to sit down

Can somebody please explain the purpose
of 'The Technical Area'? Why is it called
technical? What is remotely technical
about it? It's just some white lines painted
on the ground. As far as I can tell, it is
there purely to give managers a theatre
in which to rant and wave their arms
around. Why can't they just shout from a
seated position the way motorists do?

Some pundits maintain that players like
to see their managers throwing a tantrum
on the touchline because it demonstrates
how much they care. But how many of us
would find it a boost to our morale if our
boss strutted up and down on the edge of
our workspace screaming and throwing
his arms around? In any other industry,
the HR department would definitely send
him on a course.

The technical area was enshrined in
the laws of football in 1993. In reality,

it exists because it is good box office.
It provides an additional stage for the
soap opera. But the showy conduct of
managers is just one element of what is
perhaps the biggest change that I noticed
when watching those black-and-white
televised matches.

10. There used to be less posturing

I must have watched hundreds of hours
of footage by now, and seen countless
goals being celebrated. At no point have
I seen Nat Lofthouse make a point of
kissing the badge on his shirt or Johnny
Haynes mockingly cup his hand to his
ear to taunt opposing fans. (In fact,
the only interaction of any kind with
opposing fans that I have seen is Peter
Osgood casually flicking a V-sign at
the home fans after he scored against
Manchester City at Maine Road.) Not
once, by way of celebration, does Stanley
Matthews kick a corner flag out of the
ground or turn his back to the crowd
and proudly point to the number on the

back of his shirt. Though he scores many, many goals – some of them absolute belters – Bobby Charlton *never* tears off his shirt.

Perhaps the most depressing thought is that many modern players *rehearse* how they will celebrate in the event of their scoring a goal. That represents a fundamental change in attitude. If you go online, you can find a wonderful goal scored by Jimmy Greaves playing for Spurs against Manchester United. At astonishing speed, he glides past several bemused Man Utd defenders before rounding the keeper and tapping the ball into an empty net. By any standards, it is a very special goal. And the Spurs players celebrate, spontaneously, of course they do. Some give Jimmy a pat on the back, some shake his hand, some ruffle his hair as they all trot back towards the halfway line.

Yet week after week in the modern game, even in the lower leagues, some nonentity

of a striker taps the ball into an empty net
from three yards and then immediately
races to the corner flag and, say, starts
flapping his elbows as he dances around
pretending to be a chicken. Before you
know it, all his team-mates have formed
a circle around him and they, too, are
pretending to be chickens. Why are
spectators being subjected to this naff,
choreographed nonsense? He's a striker
who scored a goal. That is called doing
your job. There is no need to create a
special dance for just doing your job.
Imagine if you walked into Greggs
and the entire staff were moonwalking
backwards because they had just
baked a scone.

A simple change to the regulations would
fix all this. The new rule should be
that when you score a goal you have 30
seconds in which to celebrate. At the end
of 30 seconds, the other team get to kick
off regardless and if you're still up the
wrong end pretending to be chickens then
that's your lookout.

To my mind, some new rules could quickly dispose of much of these theatrics. Take the feigning of injuries, for example. For the footballer of yesterday, pretending to be injured would have been shameful. You would never see players screaming, clutching their face, rolling around or thumping the pitch in supposed agony. Quite the opposite, in fact. They would limp to their feet determined to show their opponent that they had not been cowed. Their attitude was very similar to the knight played by John Cleese in *Monty Python and the Holy Grail*.

Today's footballer, by contrast, fakes injury to try and gain an advantage. And who can blame them when the financial rewards for winning are so astronomical? We need to disincentivise these behaviours. The new rule should be that if a player is caught feigning injury then he should be given the injury he was feigning. For example, if a player is pretending to have been headbutted, then the ref nuts him. A little Taliban, perhaps, but I'm sure it would be effective.

(Incidentally, this rule change was thought up by my good friend Guy Jenkin who was, in his pomp, a no-nonsense midfielder.)

Interestingly, those who defend the posturing in modern football often roll out the word 'passion'. A player's stripping off and leaping into the crowd is an expression of 'passion'. But today's players are paid massive sums to play. The footballers of old performed week in and week out for a maximum of £20. Over the Christmas and Easter periods they would often play three games in four days. Surely that is a level of commitment that requires more 'passion'?

The truth is that many of these changes in behaviour are not exclusive to football. We live in a more individualistic world where we spend a considerable portion of our lives striking poses while we photograph ourselves. Posturing has become recreational.

People are no longer afraid of appearing 'flash'. I suppose we should not be surprised. Affluence brings many benefits, but it does give us more opportunities to wave goodbye to our dignity.

It is probably best if I draw this chapter to a close now because I appear to have turned into Sam the Eagle from *The Muppet Show*.

The Joy of Wasted Time

A FEW days ago, I did the maths. I did it 'old school': I sat down with a pencil, paper, and rubber, and tried to approximate the sum total of hours in my life that have been lost to football. Here are the results and, in defiance of my many maths teachers, I shall not show my workings. You will just have to take my word for it.

First, I estimated how much time I have spent watching football, *live*, in a football stadium, including all the obsessive childhood years, through the couple of decades when I was a season-ticket holder, right up to the occasional visits of my recent past. My estimate came out at 1,760 hours.

Next I had to add on the astonishing number of sofa-bound hours watching football on TV. All the Match of the Days, The Big Matches, the On the Balls, the Star Soccers, the Football Focuses, the Sportsnight with Colemans, the FA Cup Finals, the World Cup tournaments, the Euros, plus my endless hours of archive viewing during the Covid lockdowns (and since). At a conservative estimate, that amounted to 8,000 hours.

Then there was all the football-related mental activity, all the arguing and discussing, the thinking about football, the daydreaming and fantasising about football that consumed my every waking thought, until the tsunami of puberty crashed its chaos through the doors of my young brain. At the very cautious assumed average of ten minutes per day, I got a figure of 19,160 hours.

Now I needed to factor in the many, many hours I spent playing Subbuteo, a game of huge skill and science that involves flicking tiny plastic footballers at an implausibly large ball. As a boy, I was addicted to it. I played it incessantly – against Andy Boyce and against many similarly addicted schoolfriends – but I also played on my own, controlling both teams in rigged matches that were invariably won by Chelsea with a late wonder-goal. This was how I relaxed, lost in my own world.

As a child, I was the very lucky recipient of a hell of a lot of love, but my parents no longer got on well with each other so there was always an undercurrent of tension in the house. One of my escapes was to shuffle around for many hours on my knees, propelling miniature heroes across a crumpled, green baize pitch. In toto, my estimate was that I did this for 2,500 hours. I don't play any more. My knees would probably explode if I tried.

Finally, and most significantly, there was the sum of all the glorious hours that I have spent actually playing football. I started at the age of five in 'The Cage', a playground that was six houses away from my house. It was a magical paradise, apart from the broken glass and dog shit. Often we would play until darkness had descended and the ball was a faint white glow. If playing outside was not an option, I could play five-a-side indoors in the church hall behind our house. Dad was the caretaker, so access was not a problem. I played with the Cubs, and later the Scouts, and of course during every breaktime in the school playground, where several games involving boys of different ages all took place at once with only the occasional injury as the swarms collided.

I also played on my own, in the empty kitchen, thumping a woollen ball against the wall as I acted out yet more matches in the stadium of my imagination with me playing alongside Jimmy Greaves/Peter Osgood/Charlie Cooke/Pelé. In these matches, I always gave a very good account of myself. In fact, I was often voted Man of the Match.

In adult life, I ran a Sunday-morning team who played in a ramshackle, highly enjoyable league for many years. We had some very decent players and often played some lovely football, but we rarely kicked off on time or with the full 11 players on the pitch. Over the years, we acquired a wonderful motley crew of players that included musicians, builders, actors, journalists, fish salesmen, cartoonists, janitors, writers, sisters' boyfriends and, for a while, a Nigerian prince. At least, he said he was a prince.

For the last 30 years or so, I have played an hour of five-a-side on Friday evenings. Currently, we play on the roof of a school in South Kensington. (Don't worry, it's a flat roof.) Our game is for over-50s only and once a week a bunch of us trundle around for 60 minutes (minus water breaks) and somehow time is put into reverse and we become boys. Very slow, stiff, wheezy boys.

My estimate for time spent *playing* football is approximately 20,000 hours. So, all the subtotals aggregate to a grand total of 51,320 hours. Roughly 2,138 days. Just under six years. A fraction under 10 per cent of my life consumed, in one way or another, by football. Although for about a third of my life I have been asleep, so the percentage of my *waking* life is more like 14 per cent.

Was that time wasted? Almost certainly. Who knows what I might have achieved with that extra 14 per cent of my life? There might be peace in the Middle East by now. On the other hand, football has taught me many valuable life lessons. In no particular order they are:

1. **Keep going. Right to the end**
   On many a Sunday morning, I played in matches where we went three or four goals down before battling back to win. However, there were also many matches

where we took a three- or four-goal lead and then collapsed like a Jenga tower.

2. If you're afraid to fail, you'll never succeed

This is true in all walks of life and even more so in football. To play an imaginative, defence-splitting pass, you have to take the risk of giving the ball away, as I have had to explain to many an angry team-mate.

3. Moaning is pointless

It never changes anything and it just damages confidence, as I have pointed out to many team-mates after I have just given the ball away.

4. Confidence is transformative and mysterious

There are days when both feet feel like they belong to someone else, perhaps a drunk paraplegic. Yet there are days when you can nutmeg the Watford, AC Milan and England striker, Luther Blissett. Yes, I did that, in a charity game. Although

I have a sneaking suspicion that Luther parted his legs to let me do it, rather like a dad might do up the park.

5. Winning isn't everything

Danny Blanchflower famously said, 'The great fallacy is that the game is first and last about winning. It is nothing of the kind. The game is about glory.' Wise words from a footballing great, even if he was deluded enough to play for Spurs. Fans like to see their team win – of course they do – but, more importantly, they want their team to make them feel proud.

For a brief, disastrous spell, Danny Blanchflower managed Chelsea and demonstrated just how secondary he thought winning was.

6. Life can be cruel. Get over it

Your captain can be about to score the penalty that will win you the Champions League, when he will slip and end up on his arse. Or a referee will fail to notice a Tottenham player yanking someone to the ground by his hair. There is arbitrary injustice everywhere and sometimes you will be the beneficiary. VAR is supposed to solve this but as many instances have proved, six people can cock things up just as easily as one.

Albert Camus, the French writer and philosopher, claimed that all his moral architecture came from the lessons he learned playing as a goalkeeper. If you read *L'Étranger*, you can see that its bleak themes have been influenced by the author being repeatedly kicked in the face. There are many perceptive quotes by Camus about the life lessons of football. By contrast, the best that his fellow-existentialist Jean-Paul Sartre could come up with was 'In a football match, everything is complicated by the presence of the other team.' Hmm. I hope he didn't get paid for that.

Sixty Years On

AFTER A lifetime consumed by football, it gives me no pleasure to cast myself as this moaning Cassandra (no, that's a lie; predicting disaster is fun), but the professional game is facing a grim future. At Chelsea, I fear, that future is already here. We have become the Premier League's most conspicuous basket-case and the perfect example of everything that can go wrong once venture capitalists take charge.

When the club was acquired by a shadowy consortium, Clearlake, and its frontman, Todd Boehly, the new owners portrayed themselves as serious investors with long-term strategies and cool heads. In reality, they have behaved more like a bull in a china shop. Correction, a herd of bulls. Blind, rabid bulls. With a mixture of arrogance and recklessness, they did not pause to learn about either the club or the sport. Instead, they immediately imposed an insane business model, buying dozens of expensive players until the squad became absurdly bloated and, inevitably, impossible to manage. Apparently, the masterplan was to sell many of these players on at a profit. Well, most of them have played so little that they have completely lost their confidence and their value is plummeting. So good luck with that, Todd. With no revenues from the Champions League and the restrictions of Financial Fair Play, it seems likely that mounting losses will lead to continued failure on the pitch.

Now, being a mid-table team doesn't worry me. Chelsea have spent much of their history like that. What does worry me is being pushed over a financial precipice by a bunch of ignorant moneymen. I use the word ignorant because, so far, they have blundered into every mistake imaginable. Worse still, with every disastrous turn, Todd Boehly has come out with yet more grandiose bullshit. For all his many, many, many faults, at least Abramovich did not subject us to his opinions.

Of course, by the time this book is published, a new season will have begun and Chelsea may be prospering at the top end of the league. But that would not change my conviction that there is a sickness at the heart of the club. At the heart of many clubs, in fact. Sooner or later, elite professional football is going to have to decide whether it wants to be a sport or a pointless circus. It is going to have to address all the disturbing issues centred around ownership, hypocrisy, rapacious commercialisation and madhouse economics. There are so many big, debt-ridden clubs whose business model is based on an assumption of ever-increasing TV revenues. And while this is how a lot of business operates, no boom lasts forever. No matter how big the bubble may grow, in the end it always bursts. And what happens then? When the banks eventually lose patience and call in the debts, it could prove terminal for many clubs, especially if their bedrock supporters have been priced out and gone elsewhere looking for a more satisfying experience.

Whenever I am visiting family in the Scottish Highlands, I try to go and watch Nairn County play in the Highland League. The football is not always of the highest quality, especially when the wind is propelling the ball faster than anyone can kick it, but I always enjoy the experience because there is an atmosphere that I recognise and remember; a sense of community and place. I get the same feeling at AFC Wimbledon, a club created and owned by fans who had their original club stolen from them by foreign owners who moved it 70 miles away. Perhaps small community clubs like these are where the future of football lies, far from the toxic reach of any Glazers, Boehlys or Mohammed bin Salmans.

Or perhaps the growth in women's football points the way ahead – provided that the women's game does not end up making the same mistakes as the men's game. It was a little ominous after the final of the European Championships to hear a pundit say that England's win was particularly brilliant because it would attract bigger sponsors to the women's game. Is that really what it needs in order to be deemed a success?

At the start of this book, I wrote about how finding the scissors had become more important to me than listening to the climax of Chelsea v Newcastle. But I have to confess that, when I later watched the highlights of that game on *Match of the Day*, I *did* get excited. The bulk of the contest looked pretty dire, but Kai Havertz scored a winner in the closing minutes. What lifted me from my chair, however, was not the fact that he had scored, but the manner of it. He killed a chipped pass stone dead on his instep and then – in one continuous, fluid move – flicked the ball past the onrushing keeper with the outside of his foot. It was a moment of exquisite instinct that any true football fan would applaud because they would know they had seen something special, something that is fantastically difficult to do.

As a small boy, I fell head-over-heels in love with Chelsea and football – in that order. But as I grew up, the order flipped. Yes, for me, blue will always be the colour, but it no longer bothers me much when Chelsea lose. With the passing of the years, as you'll have gathered, I have become very disenchanted with so much of the greedy emptiness that has attached itself to professional football. But the game itself can still set my pulse racing. The joy of watching a Lionel Messi will always outweigh the cringe of listening to an Infantino.

In another 60 years' time, when – or rather *if* – Chelsea are playing Newcastle, I hope that, somewhere, there will still be an excited six-year-old, fizzing with anticipation, who is about to witness their first match, live, in a stadium full of happy people. And if that happens, I really hope it's on a Saturday.

Acknowledgements

MY GREATEST thanks are owed to Ian Ridley, who both suggested and commissioned this memoir. Without his considerable support and enthusiasm, this book would never have happened.

I am also indebted to my copy editor, Charlotte Atyeo. She helped me to iron out some of the compulsive tics and sloppy habits of my prose style.

As regards the unreliable memories I've drawn on, I've already acknowledged the role of my three main companions at all those Chelsea matches – my big brother Peter, my cousin Johnny and my friend Andy Boyce.

However, there are many others whose company I have enjoyed over the years on the terraces or in the seats at Stamford Bridge. They will all have had to put up with my constant chatter. So, in no particular order, I salute the following: Dave Whittaker, Mickey Leach, Jimmy Mulville, John Ryan, Dave Dawson (the world's nicest cabbie), Mike Richards, Peter Benfield, David and Jeremy Vooght, Bill Tidey, Tom Webber and any other fellow-sufferers whose names may have slipped down the back of my brain.

Our friend, Victoria Dannreuther, took my handwritten drafts and typed them out immaculately, as she always does.

Lastly, I must thank my wife, Libby, who has had to listen to so many of these stories and observations on so many occasions and who will probably hear them all again.

About the Author

ANDY HAMILTON is one of Britain's leading comedy writers, with a long string of credits across radio, television and film. He has also written two novels. After grammar school in London, Andy read English at Downing College, Cambridge and was a member of the University's Light Entertainment Society.

He joined the BBC in 1976, writing for radio series such as *Week Ending*, *The News Huddlines* and *The Million Pound Radio Show*. In more recent years, his Radio 4 credits, both writing and appearing, have included *Old Harry's Game*, *Revolting People*, *Trevor's World of Sport* and *Andy Hamilton Sort of Remembers*.

It is probably as a TV writer that Andy became best known. After contributing to such TV comedy

180

classic shows as *Chelmsford 123*, *Not the Nine O'Clock News* and *Alas Smith and Jones*, with Guy Jenkin he wrote the hugely successful series *Drop the Dead Donkey* for Channel 4, *Outnumbered* for the BBC and *Kate and Koji* for ITV. In addition, he wrote the TV football comedy drama *Eleven Men Against Eleven* and the cinema film *What We Did on Our Holiday*, which starred David Tennant, Rosamund Pike and Billy Connolly.

Andy is also a much-in-demand performer, touring with his stand-up show and appearing regularly on such TV shows as *Have I Got News For You* and *QI*, along with *I'm Sorry I Haven't A Clue* and *The News Quiz* on radio.

To cap it all – pun intended – and despite his diminutive stature, Andy is also the voice of Dr Elephant the dentist in the children's programme *Peppa Pig*.

Novels by Andy Hamilton

The Star Witness
(Unbound, 2016)

Longhand
(Unbound, 2020)